THE
Quotable
FULTON
J. SHEEN

Compiled and Edited
by FREDERICK GUSHURST
and the Staff of *Quote*

DROKE HOUSE, Publishers

ANDERSON, S. C.

Distributed by
GROSSET AND DUNLAP
51 Madison Avenue, New York, N. Y.

Library of Congress Catalog Card Number: 67–13273

Published by DROKE HOUSE, Publishers,
309 S. Main, Anderson, S. C.

MANUFACTURED IN THE UNITED STATES OF AMERICA
FOR DROKE HOUSE, PUBLISHERS
BY
KINGSPORT PRESS, INC., KINGSPORT, TENN.
DESIGNED BY W. J. MC INTOSH

Front Cover Photo by Louis Orsini. Back Cover Photo by H. J. Fennimore, Detroit.

*Dedicated to the LADY who looked down
to Heaven as she held Heaven in her arms.*

FULTON J. SHEEN

Contents

INTRODUCTION   vii

ACKNOWLEDGMENTS   ix

QUOTATIONS
(Arranged Alphabetically by Primary Subject)   3

THE WIT OF FULTON J. SHEEN   271

BIOGRAPHY (VITA)   283

INDEX   293

EDITORS' PAGE   313

Introduction

Bishop Sheen receives 8,000 to 10,000 letters every day. His television program has averaged a weekly audience of thirty million, competing successfully in the choicest time slots with the most popular programs. Quite obviously, therefore, it is impossible to *introduce* either the man or his work to this generation.

Simply to review his endeavors and accomplishments in the bleached form of a resumé, such as appears at the end of this book, is enough to stagger the imagination—enough to make even the most cynical wonder what it is that fires this dynamo.

In a few spare moments, in between his duties and problems as Bishop of Rochester and National Director of the principle mission organization within the entire Catholic Church, his quarter-century career as a university professor, the pressures of a newspaper column, his very important role in the Vatican Council, the preparations needed for innumerable speeches, radio programs, recordings and individual consultations, not to mention his activities simply as a priest—Bishop Sheen has managed to write, at the last count, sixty-three books.

It is from these books, and from important speeches and

articles, that I have had the privilege of selecting the material that constitutes the present book. Here, in one volume, is a fair spectrum of the succinct and penetrating, and one is tempted to say timeless thoughts, of a truly coherent mind. His theological writings are standard fare in seminaries, his philosophical works are pondered by philosophers of every persuasion, and you may be sure that diplomats both friendly and unfriendly have studied late into the night, and with care, the thoughts in this book. But I suspect it is the common people who are most obliged to Bishop Sheen, and for whom he, on his part, has had the greatest concern. His public impact on our century has been wide and deep, and cannot as yet be appraised; his true impact is secret. In dark rooms the tears of many a broken and lonely soul have stained his books.

FREDERICK GUSHURST

Acknowledgments

Appreciation is extended to His Excellency Bishop Fulton J. Sheen for his cooperation in granting to the publishers permission to use all of his words, written and spoken, in the compilation and editing of this volume.

Thanks are due also to Mr. Louis Orsini and Mr. H. J. Fennimore for permission to use the cover photos; to Sue G. Hall for the dust jacket design of the book; and to Robert T. Owens and the staff of QUOTE for their many hours of effort.

A special debt of appreciation is owed to the book's editor, Frederick Gushurst, for an outstanding job of research and selection of quotations, extracted from literally every book, newspaper column, radio talk, telecast and article by, or concerning, the subject.

WILTON HALL, JR.
Publisher
DROKE HOUSE
1967

QUOTATIONS

· · A · ·

ABUSE

Abuse never takes away the right of use. Automobiles kill people; we must not destroy automobiles. Every gift of God is capable of producing some evil through the abuse of creatures such as fire, flesh, wine. Excess of any of these constitute evils; elimination of all of them would destroy cooking, families, and conviviality. Nothing in the universe is intrinsically evil; God saw that it was good.   [1

ACTION

... **Emotion.** Good emotions that do not result in action take the edge off conscience, and draw a veil over moral visions.   [2

ACTS

... **Habits.** Sow an act and you reap a habit. Sow a habit and you reap a character. Sow a character and you reap a destiny.   [3

ADJUSTMENT

Too much emphasis is laid upon the fact that we must adjust ourselves to our environment and adjust ourselves to society. Rather, we must first be self-adjusted, by subordination of body to soul, senses to reason, reason to faith.   [4

ADVERSITY

Some people never look up until they are flat on their backs; they never think of God until they are face to face with some disaster. A great deal of rust requires a sharp file. Many a person would never think upon the meaning of life unless sickness had detached him from his great love of the foibles of this life.   [5

The springs of fresh water well up amid the brine of the salt sea, the fairest Alpine flowers bloom in the most rugged mountain passes, and the noblest songs are the outcome of the profoundest agony of soul.   [6

ADVICE

When one is in trouble, one should never go for advice to one who never says prayers or who has not passed through suffering.   [7

AFFLICTION

As snow is cold and yet warms and refreshes the earth, so afflictions and efforts at moral regeneration warm and perfect the soul. The crutch-leaners rot in honey; the cross-bearers are preserved in brine.   [8

AFFLUENCE

...Problems. Why is it that juvenile delinquency is highest in countries that are the most economically developed; why are there more psychotics and neurotics among the over-privileged than among the underprivileged? Such considerations as these make more momentous than ever the question of the Lord: "How is a man better for it, if he gains the whole world at the cost of losing his own soul?"   [9

AGE

... **Old.** Those who have a philosophy of life are not troubled with age. Our last days should be the best days. The evening praises the day; the last scene commands the act; and the music reserves its sweetest strains for the end.
[10

AGGRESSIVENESS

Each of us comes into life with fists closed, set for aggressiveness and acquisition; but when we abandon life, our hands are open; there is nothing on earth that we need, nothing the soul can take with it.   [11

AGNOSTICISM

Agnosticism is not an intellectual position, but a moral position, or better still, an intellectual defense for a life which is afraid of the light.   [12

... **Escapism.** Escapists who want a religion without a cross call themselves agnostics in order to avoid the moral consequences of truth. Agnosticism, skepticism, and cultivated doubt do not represent an intellectual position—for wherever there is a shadow there must be light, and negation would not exist if there were nothing to deny. These attitudes are rather a moral position, in which a person attempts to make himself invulnerable to divine truth by denying its existence and turning his back on it, as Pilate did.   [13

ALCOHOLISM

... **Cure.** The alcoholic must see his own powerlessness as emptiness . . . The moment, when the alcoholic perceives his powerlessness and faces the tragic fact of what he is, is very dangerous, for it could result in despair . . . Shame sometimes maddens people into frantic resistance, as the last remnants of pride recoil against detected criminality . . . The soul that had a devil driven out of it was likened to an empty house. Because good did not come to dwell in the house, seven other spirits worse than the first came to dwell there, and "the last state of the man was worse than the first." It does no good to create this emptiness and this powerlessness unless goodness is ready to move in.   [14

... **Drunkards.** The drunkard is a sinner; the alcoholic has a pathological condition with which there is associated a psychologic obsession that he must drink. The psychic obsession may come from within, but it could also come from without in the form of evil spirits. Just as there are good angels that give us good thoughts, so there are bad angels that give us evil thoughts.   [15

... **Love.** No cure for alcoholism will ever be perfect without the introduction of love . . . Alcoholism cannot be driven out; it must be crowded out.   [16

... **Pride.** The infernal pride that every alcoholic has in himself that he can cure himself in his own way and in his own good time, or else that he is not an alcoholic, must be

6

broken. Self reflection must reach a point where he says, "I am powerless over alcohol." An alcoholic must see that he, as a result of slow leaks and blowouts, is now a flat tire and cannot fix himself. [17

... **Psychic Effects.** A drunken pig is not the same as a drunken man. There is a voluntary element, at least in the beginnings of alcoholism, which is not to be associated with alcoholism which completely demarcates it from a disease. One such effect is lying. Practically all alcoholics are liars . . . an alcoholic will never admit he is an alcoholic. He may admit to his excessive drinking or drunkenness but never to alcoholism. [18

... **Reasons.** Why do people drink and become alcoholics? For one of two reasons: either because they like liquor, or because they do not like something else. [19

... **Will Power.** It does no good to tell the alcoholic that he must use his will power, for that is precisely his problem: he has no will power. [20

ALIENATION

Alienation from self and from one's fellow men has its roots in separation from God. Once the hub of the wheel, which is God, is lost, the spokes, which are men, fall apart. [21

... **Modern Man.** The modern man is characterized by three alienations: he is divided from himself, from his fellow man, and from his God. These are the same three character-

istics of the frustrated youth in the land of the Gera-
senes.   [22

AMERICA

... **Decay.** Arnold Toynbee asserts that 16 out of 19
civilizations that have decayed since the beginning of the
world up to the present have decayed from within. Lincoln
always said that America would never be conquered from
without. If it ever perishes, and please God it will not, it will
do so from within.   [23

... **Good; Evil.** If America is to continue to be great
along the tradition of her Founding Fathers and not betray
the Christian traditions, her citizens must release not their
evil inclinations from within but rather the aspiration for
total goodness that God put in their hearts.   [24

... **Heritage.** If you wish to keep your light and heat,
you must also keep your sun. If you wish to keep your
perfume, you will keep your flowers. If you wish to keep
your forests, you must keep your trees, and if you wish to
keep your rights and liberties in education, you must also
keep your God. That is the American heritage.   [25

... **Mission.** Our country has always had a great mission. In the beginning of our history we were a sanctuary for
the oppressed. In our times we became an arsenal for democracy. In the last few years we have been the pantry for the
starving   world.   [26

... **Purpose.** The United States . . . is on the defen-
sive, not only because it does not have it in its heart to wage

8

war, but also because it lacks that unity of purpose which it would have if it saw itself the defender not of political methods, but rather of the great spiritual heritage of the Hebraic-Christian tradition.   [27

... **Purpose.** The long arm of Providence is reaching out to America, saying, "Take up thy cross! The cross of all the starving people of the world. Carry it!"   [28

... **Salvation.** America will be saved, not by merely knowing how wicked are its enemies, but rather by an inner regeneration of its spirit, a restoration of family life, and a return of the people to God. Then, if God is with us, who can be against us?   [29

AMERICANISM

The essence of Americanism is not revolution, but the recognition of the sacredness of human personality, and the inherent inalienable rights which every man possesses independent of the State.   [30

AMERICANS

... **Abroad.** Every adult regrets that he did not study harder when in school. This is particularly true of Americans who visit France. They had a little "book French" in school but they never seem to speak "book French" in Paris. Americans get angry because the horses and dogs understand French, and they do not. Then the American feels that the reason the French do not understand him is because the Frenchman is deaf. So he shouts. About the only one who understands an American in France is another American.   [31

...**Values.** America is a country of ulcers, and ulcers vary in direct ratio to the number of keys on a key ring and the number of telephones on a desk. Premium is put upon doing, acting, moving, at the expense of thought . . . So much absorbed are we in action that now magazines will place under the title of the article written for relaxation 'Reading time: 8 minutes, 30 seconds'. We know of a man in New York who carries an alarm clock in a suitcase when he goes out for a walk; when the alarm clock goes off, he turns round and returns home.   [32

ANGELS

...**Belief In.** The Jews believed in angels . . . Moslems believe in angels; Christians believe in angels; and pagans believed in angels. Plutarch . . . Epictetus . . . Seneca and Virgil believed in angels. Plato and Aristotle also held that God used angels for the government of the world . . . There is room enough in the heart of a man for an angel, for an angel takes no room.   [33

...**Decisions.** Once an angel has made a decision, it can never again change its mind. In this the mind of an angel is very unlike that of a woman. It is said that a woman's mind is cleaner than a man's because she changes it more often.   [34

...**Intelligence.** The angelic intelligence is quite different from the human intelligence . . . the angel does not receive its knowledge from things. Rather, ideas are poured into the angel by God. Man knows from the bottom up; an angel knows from the top down . . . An angel knows more

science than Einstein, more baseball than Casey Stengel and
more jokes than Bob Hope.   [35

ANGER

... **Just Anger.** Of all the emotions anger alone has no
contrary emotion . . . It has been well summarized by Victor Hugo: "Pride robs me of God, envy of my neighbor, and
anger of myself." But there can be a just anger too; this is
more rare than the unjust, for just anger is controlled. Just
anger has almost vanished from the world which has lost the
distinction between right and wrong.   [36

ANONYMITY

One of the reasons why people who are calm at home are
impatient behind the steering wheel is because they know, as
they shout at other drivers, that they are unknown. They
regard anonymity as a protection of their character.   [37

ANXIETY

The complexes, anxieties, and fears of the modern soul
did not exist to such an extent in previous generations because they were shaken off and integrated in the great so-
cial-spiritual organism of Christian civilization. They are,
however, so much a part of modern man that one would
think they were tattooed on him . . . If the modern man
wants to go to God from the devil, start with the devil: that
is where the Divine Lord began with Magdalene.   [38

... **Cause.** Anxiety stems fundamentally from irregu-
lated desires, from the creature wanting something that is unnecessary for him or contrary to his nature or positively

harmful to his soul. Anxiety increases in direct ratio and proportion as man departs from God. [39

. . . **Modern.** Modern anxiety is different from the anxiety of previous and more normal ages in two ways. In other days men were anxious about their souls, but modern anxiety is principally concerned with the body; the major worries of today are economic security, health, the complexion, wealth, social prestige, and sex. [40

APATHY

Life is to be defined as the sum of forces which resist death . . . Apathy and numbness of soul are nothing else but creeping death. [41

APOSTLES' CREED

There is not a single quotation from the Gospels in the Apostles' Creed. The early Christians of the first century were recording in that Creed certain facts of which the Gospels were the literary and fuller expression. [42

APPEARANCE

. . . **Conscience.** Many a modern conscience is like a woman before her mirror. Just as soon as she sees herself, she puts on her makeup. [43

. . . **Dress.** The less grace men and women have in their souls, the more gaudily they dress. [44

APPEARANCES

Adam and Eve were not conscious of the need of clothes until after they had sinned . . . Once naked on the inside, external covering was necessary . . . the soul has its apparel as well as the body, and the psychologists are right in saying that exaggerated display on the outside is a sign of barrenness within . . . those who keep up the externals only to cover up the internal are like some of the ancient Egyptian temples that were magnificent on the outside, but on the inside had only the image of a serpent or a crocodile.

[45

APPLAUSE

I always consider applause at the beginning of a lecture a manifestation of faith. If it comes in the middle, it is a sign of hope. And if it comes at the end, it is always charity. [46

ARGUMENTS

Arguments are useless in convincing a boy he ought to like spinach. [47

ART

... Christian. When one searches for the reasons why Christian art should have pictured Joseph as aged, we discover that it was in order better to safeguard the virginity of Mary . . . this is like assuming that the best way to show that a man would never steal is to picture him without hands. [48

ASCETICISM

... Egotism. A "saint" who spends his life sizzling on hot coals or reclining on railroad spikes would never be canonized by the Church. Asceticism for asceticism's sake is actually a form of egotism, for self-discipline is only a *means,* the end of which is a greater love of God. Any form of asceticism which disrupted charity would be wrong—this was the mistake of the monk who decided to live only on crusts and upset the whole monastery, turning it into one vast crust hunt to satisfy his idiosyncrasies . . . As the perfection of the rose and not the destruction of the bush is the purpose of pruning, so union with God is the purpose of self-discipline. [49

. . . **Love.** The end of Christian living is the attainment of love, and there is a double commandment touching this love: one, to love God; the other, to love neighbor. To realize either aspect, some asceticism is required. The only way we can help ourselves to love God is by conquering our selfishness, and the only way that we can ever conquer the evil in our neighbor is by making him feel the beneficient power of our love. [50

ASSUMPTION

As a rich brother takes on himself the debt of his bankrupt brother, so Our Lord takes upon Himself all the discords, disharmonies, all the sins, guilts, and blasphemies of man, as if He Himself were guilty. [51

ATHEISM

Those who rob man of God spoil his nature. [52

. . . **Communist.** Communist atheism . . . is not a denial of God; it is rather a challenge of God. Militant atheism is an experience of God, just as much as wifebeating is an experience of marriage. All hatred is love turned upside

14

down. Whence comes the persecution, the violence, the hatred, the intensity of militant atheism if it be not the very reality of the God they attack? God is more alive in the minds of the Communist atheists as a phantom than He is in the mind of the Western world.　　　　　　　　　　[53

... Intellectual. If there is no intellectual atheism, there is a frequent atheism of the will, a deliberate rejection of God. That is why the psalmist places atheism not in the mind but in the heart: "The fool has said in his *heart,* there is no God."　　　　　　　　　　　　　　　　[54

... Modern Atheists. The modern atheist does not disbelieve because of his intellect, but because of his will; it is not knowledge that makes him an atheist, but perversity. The denial of God springs from a man's desire not to have a God—from his wish that there were no Justice behind the universe, so that his injustices would fear no retribution; from his desire that there be no Law, so that he may not be judged by it; from his wish that there were no Absolute Goodness, that he might go on sinning with impunity. That is why the modern atheist is always angered when he hears anything said about God and religion—he would be incapable of such a resentment if God were only a myth.　　[55

... Religion. Once atheism tries to confront religion with reason, atheism will lose.　　　　　　　　　　[56

... Self-Hatred. The organized atheism of the present hour is . . . a projection of self-hatred; no man hates God without first hating himself.　　　　　　　　　　　[57

15

ATHEISTS

What saves the atheist from the stigma of insanity is the fact that God is real, not like a dream but like an enemy at his door.   [58

... **Energy.** The energy of atheists, their tireless propaganda, their spirited discourses, testify to a belief in God which puts to shame mere lip worshippers. They are always thinking of God.   [59

ATOMIC BOMB

The world has abandoned God and cast its lot with nature divorced from Nature's God. Such is the meaning of the atomic bomb.   [60

It is very foolish to believe that the terrific instruments of destruction will induce men to forego war.   [61

... **Man.** The atomic bomb in the hands of a Francis of Assisi would be less harmful than a pistol in the hand of a thug; what makes the bomb dangerous is not the energy it contains, but the man who uses it.   [62

ATOMIC ENERGY

Atomic energy is a blessing, just like fire. Our worry is atomic men.   [63

AUTHORITY

... **Parental.** The authority of the parent is never abstracted from his personality; a rule is always incarnated in the person who makes it.   [64

··B··

BEAUTY

... **Soul.** Beauty on the outside never gets into the soul, but beauty of the soul reflects itself on the face. Its loveliness refuses to be imprisoned; it comes out in the eyes, the words, and the kindness of the hands. [65

BEGET

... **Make.** There is assumed, throughout the Scriptures, a difference between making and begetting: we make what is unlike us, for example, a man makes a table; but we beget what is like us, for example, a father begets a child. Inasmuch as we are made by God, we are unlike Him in His Divine Nature; inasmuch as we are begotten by God, we can become like Him, be partakers of His Nature, assume our place as His children and the heirs of the Kingdom of God. [66

BEHAVIOR

... **Doubt.** It is not doubt that causes our loose behavior as often as such behavior causes doubts. Our Lord was extremely emphatic on this point: "Anyone who acts shamefully hates the light, will not come into the light, for fear

17

that his doings will be found out. Whereas the man whose life is true comes to the light, so that his deeds may be seen for what they are, deeds done in God" (John 3:20–21). [67

... **Growth.** If an acorn could voluntarily stunt its growth by refusing the nutriment of light, chemicals and rains, so that it always remained a crooked sapling, one would have a picture of what happens to a human heart, when it spurns those graces which should contribute to its perfection. [68

... **Purpose.** The reason most minds today are upset is because they lack an over-all purpose. They accept one plan of life for Monday, another Tuesday and still another for Wednesday. They read a book on Thursday and decide that all that matters is "a good time"; Friday they hear a radio sermon and decide to "give up drinking," on Saturday the impulses of the flesh are strong again and it is concluded that "I cannot help being what I am." Whenever there is complexity, there is unhappiness; whenever there is no eventual port, there is little joy in being buffeted by the winds of the sea. [69

... **Reputation.** It is really not honor based on virtue which men seek today, but rather reputation, which is measured more by its width than by its depth. Reputation is often only popularity, and, like a breeze, it cannot be kept. You must enjoy it while it blows. It is like a ball—men generally start kicking it when it stops rolling. [70

BELIEF

... **Negation.** The world today seems much more united in its negation of belief than in its acceptance of a belief. The older generation could give you at least ten reasons for a wrong belief, such as a belief in materialism, but the modern man cannot give even one bad reason for total unbelief. [71

BEREAVEMENT

When the cold hand of death is laid upon those whom you love, and your heart seems torn in twain, climb to the Hill of Calvary to be consoled by the Mother of Sorrows who is also the Cause of our Joy. [72

BIBLE AND THE CHURCH

The Bible came out of the Church, not the Church out of the Bible. When finally the Gospels were written, they were secretarial reports of what was already believed. [73

BIRTH

... **Death.** Death is meant to be our true birth . . . Christianity, in contrast to paganism, always blesses her children's spiritual birth into eternity; in the liturgy, the day on which a saint dies is called his *natilitia,* or birthday. [74

BIRTH CONTROL

The root principle of birth-control is unsound. It is a glorification of the means and a contempt of the end; it says that the pleasure which is a means to the procreation of children is good, but the children themselves are no good. The road that leads to Rome is good, but Rome is not; the machinery of generation is good, but the product is not. In other words, to be logical, the philosophy of birth-control would commit us to a world in which trees were always blooming but never giving fruit, a world of artists who were always picking up brushes but never finishing a picture, a world full of sign-posts that were leading nowhere. In this cosmos every tree would be a barren fig-tree and for that reason would have upon it the curse of God.   [75

Birth-control is the flesh-and-blood side of Prohibition—an amendment to the human constitution stating that the enthusiasm for new life must not exceed one half of one per cent. Both are equally incapable of enforcement. There is life in wine and men will have it as long as there is life; there is joy in children and men will have them as long as men love to play. As long as men feel that drinking the vintage of God's creation is not a sin, there will be bootleggers; and as long as men feel that children are the real wine of life, there will be storks—and to call the storks bootleggers will not ease the situation any more than to call the winepeddler a bootlegger.   [76

... **The Church.** It is too often said that birth-control is wrong because the Catholic Church says it is wrong. No, birth-control is wrong because reason says it is wrong; it is the misuse and abuse of certain faculties that God has given to mankind. But because the Church alone today upholds reason, that which reason condemns is identified with what the Church condemns, and forgetting the profound rationalism that inspires her, men babble about her autocratic authority.   [77

BLESSINGS

...Complacency. We have become so complacent about blessings that, if Almighty God were to lift us up and carry us to a beautiful dining room full of choice foods, we would not thank Him for the pains unless He sat us down in a comfortable chair. [78

BODY

...Soul. The greatest of all thinkers, Thomas Aquinas, said that there is no moment in which the body and soul are in closer relation and in which there is a greater repercussion of one upon the other than in the union of husband and wife. [79

BOREDOM

He who forgets that the body is the vestment of the immortal soul is destined for boredom. [80

The most bored people in life are not the underprivileged but the overprivileged. [81

...Freud; Marx. Two of the most popular theories among the bored today are the Marxian and the Freudian. Marx holds that we are economically determined; Freud, that we are biologically determined. Despite all the talk about freedom today, the plain fact is that many are bored with freedom. That is why they are willing to surrender it to a dictator as Marxism demands or else are willing to deny any personal responsibility as Freudianism suggests, by denying moral guilt. [82

BOYS

... Girls. Boys develop aggressiveness and aptitudes through their games, which prepare them for life. They develop chivalry, daring, strength, heroism, and mastery over nature; they tend to form groups as a prelude to community living later on in life. The girls, on the contrary, develop sensitiveness, emotional qualities, refinement, ideals, and timidity in order that later on there may not be a too precocious revelation of the secret; there is also an introduction to the rhythm of the cosmos, and a reminder that they are the bearers of life and contain within themselves great mysterious and creative possibilities. This polarity is essential for life; the negative and the positive poles of electricity are created, which later on make the sparks of true love possible. If this polarization is never developed, or if there is a too frequent intermingling at an early age, there is apt to be a marring of the psychic and physical development of each sex. Timidity may not be fostered in the woman, nor chivalry in the man, while a natural reserve may be wanting in both. Before the bow and the violin are to be put together to produce music, the bow must have its moment in which it is waxed and the violin its moment when the strings are tightened. A too early association is apt to produce effeminacy, unmanliness, softness, and weakness in boys, which spoil them for life. The girls, in their turn, if there is not this polarization are apt to become impudent, boyish, and tough.

[83

BRAINWASHING

One of the most diabolical practices the world has ever known, which today is universal throughout the Communist world, is the phenomenon of brainwashing. [84

BRAVERY

... Introspection. It takes a brave man to look into the mirror of his own soul to see written there the disfigurements caused by his own misbehavior.   [85

BROTHERHOOD

Our nation will be happier and our hearts will be gayer when we discover the true brotherhood of man, but to do this we must realize that we are a race of illegitimate children unless there is also the Fatherhood of God.   [86

... Communism. The Communist error is to believe that if all people share the same property, they will therefore be brothers. This is a grave fallacy; sharing the same apple does not make men brothers, but if men are brothers, they will share the same apple.   [87

... Comraderie. Men may be comrades because they belong to the same class, but men are brothers only because they have a common Father. It is that way in the family; it is that way in the world; the brotherhood of man is impossible without the Fatherhood of God.   [88

BURDENS

As soon as we protest that our burdens are too heavy, we immediately unfit ourselves for them, make them more formidable than before and ourselves less competent to do them.   [89

··C··

CALAMITY

...Worth. When calamity strikes the flint of human hearts, sparks of sacred fire are kindled and men will normally begin to make an estimate of their true worth. [90

CAPITAL

...Labor. It used to be that capital and labor were like a husband and wife, throwing dishes at each other in the privacy of their home. But now the conflicts of capital and labor are like a husband and wife shooting at each other on the street; they are injuring property, endangering life and disturbing the peace . . . The national good does not exist for them; they exist for the national good. Hence there should be found some way of settling these disputes somewhat like other disputes are settled. If two persons quarrel on a street, a magistrate settles the case; domestic courts settle family quarrels; civil courts settle disputes between social and business bodies; international courts adjudicate between nations; the only collectivity which is allowed to throw a nation into confusion is capital and labor. What is bigger than either is humanity and they must bow down in their particular egotisms to the common good. [91

CAPITALISM

At least under monopolistic capitalism and the worst forms of it, a man can leave one job and go to another, but in Russia there is only one boss.   [92

... **Monopolistic.** A monopolistic capitalism, as defined by the Papal Encyclicals, which freezes credit, concentrates wealth in the hands of the few, excludes labor from a share in the profits, and considers the right to property as so absolute as to be unbounded by its use, is not worth preserving.   [93

CHANGE

There is change, but the change is in *creatures* and not in God. Creation is an eternal act which terminates at its object when God wills it. If there is anything new in God, it is only a logical relation and even that is from our point of view . . . A king, for example, decides to make war within a year. When a year comes, the war is carried on without the least change in the will of the king, his resolution remaining the same as during the preceding year. There is a change, but the change is wholly on the part of the soldiers.   [94

CHARACTER

... **Environment.** It is vain to try to prevent evil by completely withdrawing opportunities unless one first purifies the heart. The secret, then, is not to change environment but to change character; if we change character, we change environment.   [95

...Experience. There is a great fallacy behind the belief that it is experience, pure and unalloyed, which makes character. Aristotle very wisely said that the spiritual education must be the start in order that there may be the correct interpretation of life. [96

...Psychology. There is a tendency today in certain quarters to believe that character is made by some single act in the past, and so you go back to the day when you were locked in the closet during the terrible thunder storm when your Aunt Mamie called. That was the day you began to hate your mother, and you grew up with that terrible hatred and all the complexes that you have since are due to that one single instance. Character is not made by a single act in the past. Character is made by . . . repeated acts directed toward a certain end or purpose. If the end is bad, then you have an evil character. If the end is good, then you have a good character. [97

...Selfishness. Character is like chiseling a statue; one has to knock off huge hunks of selfishness, which requires self-discipline. Only then does character begin to emerge. [98

CHILDREN

Every child is a blank parchment; you write the first few chapters of his life; he completes what you have begun. [99

...Behavior. No child is ever born a skeptic or an agnostic. Agnostics and skeptics are made not by thinking, but rather by behavior, that is, bad behavior. [100

... Broken Homes. The child in a broken home quickly learns that he does not count. A child is much wiser than the parents suspect; though there be no knowledge of God in a taught or a rational way, every child instinctively feels that his parents are representatives of God. He knows that by some law quite beyond him, he should come first in the parents love; with the innocent egotism of babyhood, he accepts his kingship as his right.   [101

... Development. What has happened before the fifteenth year is very much like the dripping of water on a winter day. If the water is clear, the icicle will be clear; if dirty, the icicle will be dirty.   [102

... Discipline. Sometimes too much is expected of children because it is thought that they will become perfect blocks of marble and images of a man, without a chisel ever knocking off huge bits of egotism. The child may be thoughtless, but the parents must not be; the child may be selfish, but the parents must be selfless. It is these "holy terrors" which make both our great men and our delinquents and criminals. The latter are terrors because the parents forgot the holy.   [103

... Duplicity. Children do not have duplicity because they are natural and it is acquired. If their mother tells them to tell a stranger at the door that she is not at home, they will invariably say, "My mother told me to tell you that she is not at home."   [104

... Hatred. Children may grow up to hate because they are hated.   [105

...Parental Failure. A child will grow up not only cynical about women if his mother failed, or cynical about men if the father failed, but particularly cynical about God and religion. He grows up with a grudge against the divine. God should have been in his home, but his parents failed their trust; therefore he will revenge himself on God. From his rank come the future persecuters of religion. [106

...Parental Training. No one ever says to a little pig, "What kind of a hog are you going to be when you grow up?" But one does ask a child, "What kind of man are you going to be?" Children are either trained by us toward a fixed goal and destiny, or they are trained in spite of us. The parents never have the alternative of deciding whether their child's mind will be full or empty. It cannot be kept empty; it will be filled with something. [107

...Parent-Child Relationship. The secret of the parent-child relationship is for the parent to say to the child: "I ask for obedience, because I am responsible to God for you." The child, in his turn, should say to himself: "In obeying my parents I am obeying God, for they take His place in my home." [108

...Parents. When a child is given to his parents, a crown is made for that child in Heaven, and woe to the parents who raise a child without consciousness of that eternal crown! [109

...Rules. Coddling parents forget that children love rules . . . The purpose of rules is not to restrain the child but to protect him against himself. [110

28

... Sensitivity. Children are basically egotistic; that is one of the reasons why they hate to be laughed at. Extreme sensitiveness characterizes their every move.   [111

... Teaching. A child is like an octopus. Its arms will reach out for something, whether that something be food or poison. Radio, television, alleys, servants, playgrounds, pictures, books—all are teachers . . . A mother would not allow her child to eat from a garbage can, and yet when that garbage is translated into evil for the mind, there is no shirking from its reception.   [112

CHILDREN OF GOD

There is a world of difference between being a creature of God and a child of God. We are made creatures of God; we *become* children of God by being reborn or begotten of Him.
[113

CHOICE

... Cross. Every man is on a cross. Some ask to be taken down like the thief on the left; others ask to be taken up like the thief on the right.   [114

CHRIST

He who came to this earth to teach us the divine sense of humor showed us everything that was lovely and beautiful in His character—except one thing. He showed us His power; He showed us His wisdom; He showed us His melting kindness; He showed us His sorrow; He showed us His tears; He showed us His forgiveness; He showed us His power over nature; He showed us His knowledge of human hearts; but there was one thing that He did not show; there was one thing He saved for those who do not take this world too seriously; there was one thing He saved for paradise; there was one thing He saved for those who, like poets and saints, have a divine sense of humor; there was one thing He saved for heaven that will make heaven heaven, and that was—His smile! [115

...Body of. If you asked me what the body of Christ means to me, I would say: "I believe that it is the temple of love, in which I am a living stone, the cornerstone of which is Christ; it is the tree of eternal life, of which I am a branch; it is the body of Christ on earth since His Ascension into heaven, and I am one of the cells of that body." [116

...Denial Of Existence. Those who would deny that Christ ever existed have to date their denial as 1940 or 1950 or 1960 years after the birth of Christ. [117

..."Good Man". Christ is not just a good man, because good men do not lie. And He lied if He is not what He claimed to be; the Son of God. Either He is the Son of God Incarnate or He is the archknave of all times, but He is not 'one of the moral teachers'. [118

...His Death. The only time that Our Blessed Lord ever is recorded as having sung is the night that He went out to His death. [119

...History. Edersheim in his *Life and Times of Jesus the Messias* enumerates 456 texts of the Old Testament which the Rabbis interpreted as referring to the Messias. From an historical point of view alone, here is uniqueness which sets Christ apart from all other founders of world religions. And once the fulfillment of these prophecies did historically take place in the person of Christ, not only did all prophecies cease in Israel, but there was discontinuance of sacrifices (a fact foretold by Daniel) when the true Paschal Lamb was sacrificed.   [120

... **Incarnation.** He who is born without a mother in heaven is born without a father on earth. He who made His mother is born of His mother. He who made all flesh is born of flesh. "The bird that built the nest is hatched therein." Maker of the sun, under the sun; Moulder of the earth, on the earth; ineffably wise, a little infant. Filling the world, lying in a manger; ruling the stars, suckling a breast; the mirth of Heaven weeps; God becomes man; creator a creature. Rich become poor, divinity incarnate; majesty subjugated; liberty captive; eternity time; master a servant, truth accused; judge judged; justice condemned; Lord scourged; power bound with ropes; king crowned with thorns; salvation wounded; Life dead. "The eternal word is dumb." Marvel of marvels! Union of unions! three mysterious unions in one: divinity and humanity; virginity and fecundity; faith and the heart of man. And though we shall live on through eternity, eternity will not be long enough for us to understand the mystery of that "Child who was a father and of the mother who was a child."   [121

... **Life.** If Our Divine Saviour had remained on earth . . . He would be only an example to be copied, a

31

voice to be heard. But once He ascended into Heaven and sent His Spirit to us, then He ceased to be only a model to be copied and became a Life to be lived. [122

... **Pre-existence.** The Person who assumed human nature was not created, as is the case of all other persons. His Person was the pre-existent Word or *Logos.* His human nature, on the other hand, was derived from the Miraculous Conception by Mary, in which the divine overshadowing of the Spirit and the human *Fiat,* or the consent of a woman, were most beautifully blended. This is the beginning of a new humanity out of the material of the fallen race. [123

... **Pre-existence.** As God preexisted His Own Mother somewhat in the way that an artist preexists his work, we can understand why she should be the Madonna of the World. Then, when He took on human flesh and became a Babe, we can understand why He climbed up her body as an ivory tower, to kiss upon her lips a Mystic Rose. [124

... **Pre-Historical.** A most important point concerning the transcendence of Christianity is that no other religion in the world had a founder who has a pre-history. No one ever knew that Buddha was coming, or Confucius, or founders of other religions, including those being inaugurated this afternoon in Los Angeles. [125

... **Savior.** If we had never sinned, we never could call Christ Savior. [126

... **Son Of Man.** Christ's title "The Son of Man" meant that He was representative not of the Jews alone, nor of the

Samaritans alone, but of all mankind . . . in order to be a sanctifier, Our Blessed Lord had to be a man like His unholy brethren. He would make them holy by reproducing in His life the lost ideal of human character and bringing that ideal to bear on their minds and hearts.   [127

... **Teachings.** What He taught was self-crucifixion: to love those who hate us; to pluck out eyes and cut off arms in order to prevent sinning; to be clean on the inside when the passions clamor for satisfaction on the outside; to forgive those who would put us to death; to overcome evil with good; to bless those who curse us; to stop mouthing freedom until we have justice, truth and love of God in our hearts as the condition of freedom; to live in the world and still keep oneself unpolluted from it; to deny ourselves sometimes legitimate pleasures in order the better to crucify our egotism—all this is to sentence the old man in us to death. [128

... **Truth Of.** Do you really believe that this divine Truth would come to this earth, speak a few words, and allow them to be wafted away by a Galilean breeze? It is absurd to believe that He Who wrote only once in His life, and that was in the sands, and Who never told anyone to write, should have intended that His truth should be available only and exclusively in a few memoranda that were written down by a few followers over twenty years after His death, and were never gathered together in their approved form until three centuries later. Grant that they are inspired and revealed, and I believe it and confess it and read those writings daily; but I still say it is unthinkable that these books which were not written until His Mystical Body was

33

already spread throughout the whole Roman Empire, should be *His only way* of communicating truth. If He did not take some effective guarantee to preserve His truth, which was so sacred that He died for it, then truth did not matter to Him. If He could not prolong His truth, up to this hour, then He is not God. Either that infallible truth of Jesus Christ is living now, available now, or He is not God.   [129

CHRISTIANITY

In all other religions, one has to be good to come to God—in Christianity, one does not. Christianity might be described as a "come as you are" party. It bids us stop worrying about ourselves, stop concentrating on our faults and our failings, and thrust them upon the Savior with a firm resolve of amendment.   [130

... **Cornerstone.**   Babylon, Carthage, Rome, Athens have had their spring and summer and then their winter of discontent and death; but Christianity is something that is always dying to be reborn. The bells are constantly being tolled for its execution—which never takes place. This is because Christianity is founded upon the fact that Someone was crucified and found His way out of a grave. The stone which the builders rejected is everlastingly being remade the head of the corner.   [131

... **East; West.**   Christianity, because it is outside the civilizations of the East and West, is alone capable of uniting both. Western civilization is practical. In it man does everything. God does nothing . . . Eastern civilization is mystical. God does everything, man does nothing . . . Because of its position, Christianity alone is capable of building "One World" by serving as a mediator between both, as it mediates man and the universe, this world and the next. [132

... **Freedom.** Christianity . . . postulates the fulfillment of history through the agency of free spirits. Because Christianity admits freedom, it alone admits Providence and denies fatality. It was not until the advent of Christianity with its goal beyond this world, that history was ever interpreted in terms of freedom. [133

... **Politics.** For the first time in Christian history, politics which began by divorcing itself from morality and religion, has seen that man cannot live by bread alone. So it has attempted to capture his soul, by every word that proceedeth from the mouth of a dictator. For the first time in Western Christian civilization the kingdom of antigod has acquired political form and social substance and stands over against Christianity as a counterchurch with its own dogmas, its own scriptures, its own infallibility, its own hierarchy, its own visible head, its own missionaries, and its own invisible head—too terrible to be named. [134

... **Russia.** When Russia discovers the Faith, it will sweep throughout the entire Western world; then we will know that Christianity has not failed! [135

... **Secularization.** Why are we deluged with books about the "secularization of Christianity"? Because the world cannot see any great difference between the way we act and the way it acts. No one can influence the world who is too identified with it. [136

35

...Sinners.　In other religions, one must be purified before he can knock at the door; in Christianity, one knocks on the door as a sinner, and He Who answers to us heals.

[137

...Supernatural Character.　It is an extremely unscientific approach to begin all discussion of Christianity with a denial of its supernatural character. Christianity presents itself as supernatural, and must be investigated as such. It would be quite unscientific when face to face with a person who said he was British to begin with the assumption that there are no British.

[138

...Virgin Mary.　All other world religions are lost in myth and legend except Christianity. Christ is cut off from all the gods of paganism because He is tied to woman and to history. "Born of the Virgin Mary; suffered under Pontius Pilate." Coventry Patmore rightly calls Mary: "Our only savior from an abstract Christ."

[139

...Western.　Because Western Christianity has taken Christ without the Cross, it has equated Christianity with kindness. It does not want His scarred Hands preaching sacrifice, but wants the lily-white hands of a teacher . . . A Christ without His Cross is a Christianity without sacrifice, without self-discipline; it is romanticism, sentimentalism, a mouthing of moral platitudes with petty resistance to evil and absolutely devoid of moral indignation that picks up cords and drives buyers and sellers out of temples. It is no wonder that in a streak of false broadmindedness, the Western world has identified Christ with Buddha, for Buddha had no cross either.

[140

...World. Christianity renounces the world only insofar as it is a power for evil, but it affirms the world inasmuch as it was made by God and moves toward God . . . The incarnation starts with the assumption that the disordered elements of the material universe can be reordered to serve God's purposes. For that reason Christ commanded His followers to 'preach the Gospel to every creature'—not just to every man. [141

CHRISTIAN MORALITY

...Statistics. Sex fanatics are not only nonreligious persons, but usually antireligious persons. It is curious to hear such men urge that we ought to repudiate Christian morality and develop a new ethics to suit the unethical lives of a few thousand individuals they have polled. Because statisticians can find 5000 living carnal lives, it is suggested that their ideal shall be made the universal ideal. An equal number of cases of lockjaw could be found in the United States; one wonders if lockjaw should therefore be made a physical standard of health? [142

CHRISTIANS

It is shockingly true that there is more in common today between a Christian in the state of grace, and a Chinaman, or Orthodox Jew, or a Mohammedan than there is between the true Christian and the average so-called Christian person you are apt to meet at a night club, or even at the table in your neighbor's house. [143

...Pagans. The Christian is always bound to have a great advantage over the indifferent modern pagan, simply because he knows where he is going, whereas the modern pagan knows nothing. The pagan must always be the pessimist, for he must always feel that this life is too short to give a man a chance, and the Christian will always be the optimist, for he knows that this life is long enough to give a man a chance for eternity. That is why the Christian can be joyful. That is why the pagan is sad and depressed.   [144

... **Psychoanalysis.** The Christian has no quarrel with the psychoanalyst who says that the mind of man is very much like a flower, which has roots in the mud and slime and dirt of the earth; but he will quarrel with the psychoanalyst who, concentrating upon the roots, denies the existence of the stem, the organic relationship of the leaves to the stem, or the flower's beauty. As the root is not the whole flower, so man is not wholly to be understood in terms of his unconscious.   [145

CHRISTMAS

Christmas is not something that happened such as the Battle of Waterloo; it is something that is happening.   [146

The simple shepherds heard the voice of an angel and found their Lamb; the wise men saw the light of a star, and found their Wisdom.   [147

Christmas, if it means anything, means the exaltation and glorification of the spirit of the child, which is just another word for humility.   [148

... **Good Will.** The message of the angels on Christmas night told us that only men with good will would become

God's friends. This good-will factor is so important that it seems probable there is no such thing as intellectual atheism. Reason is on God's side, not the Devil's; and to deny His absolute is to affirm a competing absolute. [149

THE CHURCH

The unity of the faithful in Christ's Body is not organizational, although an organization is necessary, and although those who admire the Church for its unity of belief and faith and liturgy attribute this to its organization. The Church is, rather, an organism. As a human body is one because it has one soul, one visible head, and one invisible mind, so the Church, the Mystical Body of Christ, is one because it has one soul—the Holy Spirit of God—one visible Head—Peter and his successors—and one invisible Head—Christ. As Christ took upon Himself a human nature from the womb of His Mother (overshadowed by the Holy Spirit), so He took from the womb of humanity (overshadowed by the Pentecostal Spirit) His Mystical Body, the Church. [150

... **Authority.** Spiritual authority is not a dam to the river of thought, it is merely a levee which prevents thought from becoming riotous and destroying the countryside of sanity. [151

... **Definition.** The Church is the *Totus Christus,* the Whole Christ, and it complements the individual Christ. In its physical aspect Christ's Body is perfect, but in its mystical aspect it is merely growing to perfection, for now it includes not only Him but us, with our imperfections. [152

... Definition. When I am asked what the Church means to me, I answer that it is the Temple of Life in which I am a living stone; it is the Tree of Eternal Fruit of which I am a branch; it is the Mystical Body of Christ on earth of which I am a member.   [153

... Enemies Of. Christ's church will be attacked, scorned, and ridiculed, but it will never be destroyed. The enemies of God will never be able to dethrone the heavens of God, nor to empty the tabernacles of their Eucharistic Lord, nor to cut off all absolving hands, but they may devastate the earth.   [154

... "Fathers, Mothers, Sisters, Brothers." In that larger family of the Kingdom of God, the priest is called "Father"—because he had begotten children not in the flesh, but in the spirit. That is why the superior of a religious community of women is called "Mother"—she has her little flock in Christ. That too is why certain teaching orders of men are called "Brothers," and why women bound in religious life by the vow of Chastity are called "Sisters."   [155

... Money. Cornelius a Lapside tells how Thomas Aquinas called upon a churchman when he was counting money. "Do you see, Thomas," said the churchman, "the church can no longer say, 'Silver and gold I have none'?" Answered Aquinas: "Neither can the church say, 'Arise and walk.'"
[156

... New Testament. Christ is living now! He is teaching now, governing now, sanctifying now—as He did in

Judea and Galilee. His Mystical Body or the church existed throughout the Roman Empire before a single one of the Gospels had been written. It was the New Testament that came out of the Church, not the Church which came out of the New Testament.   [157

... Rebels. Let not those who boast they are Catholics point their fingers at the Church in the United States, saying: "See what you are doing; see how you sin against freedom!" Whose Church is this anyway? It is OURS—yours and mine. Any bit of torn flesh in the Mystical Body of Christ is my own lacerated skin. We have too many stonecasters and not enough breast-beaters. This is our Christ! Our Church! These are our Priests! Our Sisters! Our brethren! We all fail if any one of them fails. Enough hawking up phlegm to spit in the face of Christ! Every neglect of the fatherless, the hungry, every refusal to aid in spreading the Gospel in disinherited lands is putting the purple robe on Christ again. Oh Lord! Help us put down the scourge and apply it to our own Cross-less shoulders and our unscourged back. Be the right kind of rebel.   [158

... State. The authority of civil government comes from God and must be obeyed. If a persecution against (the Roman Catholic Church) ever began in the United States, we would still be obliged to respect the government and not revolt against it.   [159

CIRCUMSTANCES

Only in a limited sense is it true that circumstances make a man; they make a man only to the extent that a man permits circumstances to make him. It is not so much the outward that influences the inward, as the inward that influences the outward. [160

CIVILIZATION

... Modern. The bald fact the enemies of God must face is that modern civilization has conquered the world but in doing so has lost its soul, and in losing its soul it will lose the very world it gained. [161

... Modern. Never before in the history of Christian civilization was there ever such a mass attack on decency, honor, personal rights and freedom as there is at the present hour . . . a civilization can be forgiven for seeing the dark side of evil, but should it not examine its conscience when it begins to fear the dark side of the good? [162

THE CLOISTERED

The cloistered men and women are doing more for our country than all its politicians, its labor leaders, its army and navy put together; they are atoning for sins of us all. They are averting the just wrath of God, repairing the broken fences of those who sin and pray not, rebel and atone not. As ten just men would have saved Sodom and Gomorrah, so ten just saints can save a nation now. [163

COLLEGES

... Curriculum. Colleges offer hundreds of courses. A college catalogue we saw not very long ago had twenty-nine distinct courses on public speaking. There are not twenty-nine different things to say about public speaking . . . I

asked the Dean, "Why do you have twenty-nine courses?"
His answer was, "Other universities do."   [164

COMMUNION

Communion is fellowship with the entire Mystical Body
of Christ. We are not to think that communion is just a
personal union between Christ and the Soul . . . for it is
there that "all who eat one Bread are one Body." The Eucharist is a greater leveller than death; it dissolves all boundaries,
nationalities and races into a supernatural fellowship where
all men are brothers of the divine Son and adopted sons of
the heavenly Father.   [165

COMMUNISM

If we see Communism as a judgment on ourselves, we
shall be more humble before God and better equipped to
resist it. It is at one and the same time an *effect* and also a
judgment on our Western world. Communism has its role to
play. Communism is not garbage; it is manure, a fertilizer. A
death is spread on the world in this our winter of discontent,
unconsciously preparing the new life for a better springtime,
when the world finally finds its way back again to God.
Communism will never be destroyed by war; it will be
converted; evil can be overcome only by good.   [166

. . . **America.**   There is considerable confusion in our
American life about Communism; too much emotional
hatred of Communism, and not sufficient thinking and reasoning about it.   [167

. . . **Appeal Of.**   Communism makes inroads because of
the vacuum created in the Western world through its loss of

faith in God. One need only notice the type of soul to which Communism appeals in our own civilization, and one finds a suggestion of the type of civilization to which it will appeal.

[168

...Conscience. There are some who enter social work in order to escape the incessant accusing repartee of their consciences . . . This group swallows the Communist line . . . because its anti-religious character satisfies their desire to expunge from the world all ideas of morality and virtue, the infractions against which have made them so uneasy in the dark.

[169

...Individuals. Communism pledges itself to be the salvation of the poor. It meets poverty in theory but does nothing in fact. One of the reasons for this is it loves the "masses" but not the poor. It has settled on an abstraction for worship, as did the French Revolution, which worshiped "humanity"; but there is no such thing as humanity, so neither are there masses; there are only individual persons.

[170

...Individuals; Religion. Karl Marx, who is the father of Communism, said, "We have already destroyed the outer religion; now we must destroy the inner religion," that is, man's spiritual nature . . . Marx said that democracy is founded on the principle of the "sovereign worth of a person." "This, in its turn," he continued, "is based upon a postulate, a dream and an illusion of Christianity, namely, that every man has an immortal soul." In the first edition of his work on capital, Marx says, "Persons of and by themselves have no value." . . . We must recognize the evil of this Communist philosophy and begin affirming, in the United States, the worth of a person as a creature of God. As Hitler put the emphasis upon *race,* as Mussolini put it on the *nation,* so the Communists put it on a *revolutionary mass.* The hour has struck to affirm the power and worth and vocation of the individual. That means returning to what Marx rightly saw as the basis of democracy, namely, the truth that every man has an immortal soul. . . . The Lord of the Universe saw value in the lowest kind of criminal and addressed him in the second person singular: "This day Thou shalt be with Me in Paradise." This promise was the foundation stone of democracy. [171

... **Injustice.** Communism is strong only when it borrows some of the moral indignation that has been inherited from the Hebraic-Christian traditions; Communism is weak when it departs from that tradition. Communism has bootlegged and smuggled into its system the decency and morality that have come from the great Hebraic-Christian tradition of the Western world and then uses it to pass judgment on the world. Moral indignation is needed against injustice, but Communists have no basis for using it. [172

... **Intellectuals.** Intellectuals do not become Communists for an intellectual reason. That is why when discussing Communism with them, they never seem to understand it. [173

... **Language Of.** Communists are speaking to the rest of the world on the basis of ethics, which their system repudiates. We, who have moral ideals, are speaking to the rest of the world in terms of economics. They are using the language that we ought to be using. [174

... **Mothers.** There is no greater refutation of Communism in the world than a mother. Because Communism denies the value of persons, it affirms that we are like grapes who have no other destiny than to have our life ground out of us for the sake of the collective wine of the state. Every mother arises to protest and proclaim, "This child of mine is a person and may not be submerged in any totality of a class or a state or a race; he is unique; he has a name; he is my son!" [175

... **Neurotics.** As flies go to honey, so neurotics gravitate to Communism. As neurotics gain stability and sanity, they leave it. [176

... **Origin.** Communism is not Russian in origin; it is Western. It belongs to Western civilization. This is a horrible thought—the more horrible because it is true. Communist philosophy is nothing but a hodgepodge, a potpourri, a melange, a mixture of all of the cheap, deistic, skeptical, rationalistic, atheistic thinking of the eighteenth and nineteenth centuries. It is a product and a judgment of the Western thinking; a judgment, because it comes back to haunt us with its evil. [177

... **Origin.** Communism came out of our Western civilization; it was produced out of what was putrid, foul, and rotten in the atheism and materialism of the nineteenth century. [178

...Purpose. It may very well be that the purpose of Communism in the modern world is to break the hard shell of materialism that is encrusting modern civilization, in order that the hidden life may spring forth unto a richer and a better culture. That may be under Providence the mission of Communism. [179

...Suppression. Thirty-seven out of every 100 people in the world today are either being pounded by the hammer or cut by the sickle. [180

COMMUNISTS
...Capitalists. The luxury and the wealth with which Soviet leaders have cast themselves is a proof that, in the long run, every Communist is nothing but a Capitalist without any cash in his pocket. [181

COMPANIONSHIP
Man is always better if he lives in companionship with those who have higher ideals; he is always worse when his companionship is with inferiors . . . Each human would be nobler in his activity and happier in his heart if, instead of seeking to keep up with the Joneses, he sought to live up to the illumination of his own personal angel. [182

COMPARATIVE RELIGION
Without denying the great contributions which the science of comparative religion has made to the general fund of knowledge, it still remains true that no science has ever been so much abused and distorted by those who bear a prejudice either to natural religion in general, or to Christianity in particular. [183

. . . Philosophy. It has been a short step for many philosophers who abuse the comparative method to argue that simply because religions are like one another, there is, therefore, no such thing as religion. That is just like saying that because hats are of different shapes, there is no such thing as a hat.   [184

COMPASSION

It is not enough merely to have an intellectual understanding of another man's difficulty; we need to go a little farther to feel it as our own burden, as the Samaritan put the wounded man upon a beast of burden and took him to an inn.   [185

. . . Involvement. Not long ago one of the nationally known picture magazines had a photograph of a man prostrate on subway stairs. For thirty minutes many people passed him by without offering a helping hand. The editorial comment was about the coldness of the modern man in the face of distress. What was forgotten was that the photographer of the picture magazine did nothing for thirty minutes for the afflicted individual except to snap pictures and make his own living.   [186

COMPLACENCY

The very moment we grow complacent about our work, our work spoils in our hands.   [187

COMPLEXES

. . . Temptation. Those who say we create "complexes" by resisting our lower nature forget that a complex is not set

up by resisting a temptation, but rather by yielding to it.
[188

CONDESCENSION

The help we give others is often condescension. We look upon them as being in need, we being the suppliers. Heaven may look upon them, however, in a different way. It may be we who are in need, not the hungry and the naked.   [189

CONFESSION

A few decades ago, nobody believed in the confession of sins except the Church. Today everyone believes in confession, with this difference: some believe in confessing their own sins; others believe in confessing other people's sins.
[190

... **Modern Man.** What shall these poor, frustrated, psychotic, and neurotic millions in our midst do to escape a creeping insanity and a growing madness? The only answer for them is to enter into themselves, to lift their eyes to the Divine Physician and cry, "Have mercy on me, O God!" If they only knew it, a single confession would rescue them by helping them to have their sins forgiven; it would also save them the small fortune spent in having their sins explained away.   [191

CONFLICT

In the Old Testament, the conflict was between the chosen people under God, and the Gentiles. In the New Testament, the conflict is more spiritual and becomes a struggle between the Beast and the Woman as revealed in the Apocalypse, and Christ and anti-Christ in the Gospels.   [192

The conflict of the future is between the absolute who is the God-man and the absolute which is the man-God; the God who became man and the man who makes himself God; between brothers in Christ and comrades in anti-Christ.

[193

...**Inner.** Too often an inner conflict is identified with the abnormal. This assumption is quite unwarranted. There are some conflicts that are normal, such as the tension we feel between the aspirations of the spirit and the carnal urges of the body; then, too, there is a conflict between what we are and what we ought to be. Tension is normal in our present human condition; it is the denial of the true causes of tension which begets so many abnormal and subhuman states.

[194

...**Inner.** A soul with a fight inside itself will soon have a fight outside itself with others.

[195

...**Man.** The intellectual world has suddenly rediscovered that man is a seat of conflict. Marx found conflict in society, Kierkegaard in the soul, Heidegger in man's being, and psychologists in the mind. To the credit of all of them, it must be said that they come much closer to an understanding of man than did the Liberals of the last few centuries who taught that man was naturally good and progressive and on the high road to becoming a god without God.

[196

...**Tension.** Conflict and tension are deeply rooted in our nature, because we are composed of body and soul, matter and spirit. Those who would escape tension altogether forget that tension is a part of our human nature as it is presently constituted. [197

CONFORMITY

... **High School.** Ever notice, when a high school empties, that almost all girls are dressed alike? A few dress a certain way, and almost everyone follows. [198

CONFUSION

... **Personality.** He was self-estranged, for when Our Lord asked, "What is thy name?" the young man answered, "My name is Legion, for we are many" . . . No divided personality is happy. The Gospel describes this unhappiness by saying that the young man was "crying and cutting himself with stones." The confused man is always sad; he is his own worst enemy, as he abuses the purpose of nature for his own destruction. [199

CONSCIENCE

... **Denial Of.** Any denial of conscience as the voice of God may be momentarily effective, but a day will come when the abused conscience will turn with fury and will harass its victim, tormenting his waking life and making his dreams a poison, his darkness a nightmare. When night gives our inner vision scope, the guilty conscience lies awake, fearful of being known in all its ugliness. There is nothing that so arouses unhealthy fear as a hidden guilt. [200

... **Examination Of.** One of the most universal spiritual practices of every saintly soul has been what is known as the nightly examination of conscience. [201

51

. . . Examination Of. Every person has a little corner in his heart he never wants anyone to venture into, even with a candle. That is why we can deceive ourselves and why our neighbors know us better than we know ourselves. The examination of unconsciousness, if it is used as a substitute for examination of conscience, only intensifies this deceit. We often justify ourselves by saying that we *are* following our consciences, when we are only following our desires. We fit a creed to the way we live, rather than the way we live to a creed; we suit religion to our actions, rather than actions to religion.   [202

. . . Guilt. If I do wrong, it fills me with a sense of guilt from which there is no escape; if the inmost sanctuary of my being is assaulted by the stern voice of this judge, I am driven out of myself by myself. Whence, then, can I fly but to myself with the sickening sense of guilt, remorse, and disgrace, which is the very hell of the soul? If, on the contrary, conscience approves my action, then there settles upon me, like the quiet of an evening dew, the joy which is a stranger to the passing pleasures of sense.   [203

. . . Power Of. If the law of conscience were of my own making, I would unmake it; but I cannot do this . . . When my will is set against hearing it, or even obeying it, it comes as a delegate with absolute right to rule over me.   [204

. . . Science. Modern science has explored the whole surface of the earth, made the sea reveal the secrets of its

depths, the sun tell the story of its wanderings, and the stars
the mystery of their light—but all this exploration is external. Modern man has done little to explore that region which
is nearest to him, and yet most unknown, namely, the depths
of his own conscience. [205

CONTEMPLATION

...**Meditation.** It is only the quiet pool that reflects the
stars. [206

...**Solitary.** Only in solitariness is true spirituality born,
when the soul stands naked before its God. In that moment
these are the only two realities in the universe. In this
discovery is born love of neighbor, for then one loves his
fellow man, not because of what he can do for us, but
because one sees that he too is a real or potential child of
God. Though truth is not personal, we make it personal by
contemplation. [207

CONVERSION

Anyone who turns his face toward the light will be converted. [208

Every soul in the world has a price tag on it, and since
many cannot or will not pay the price themselves, others
must do it for them. There is probably no other way to
account for the conversion of some souls than the fact that in
this world, as in the next, their parents, relatives, or friends
interceded to God and won for them the prize of everlasting
life. [209

... Beginning. There is one simple way of beginning a conversion: cease asking what God will give you if you come to Him, and begin to ask what you will give God. [210

... Converts. The convert no longer regrets what he might have been; the Holy Spirit fills his soul with a constant presentment of what he can become through grace. This spiritual recuperation is accompanied by hope, at no matter what age the change occurs—although the convert always regrets that he waited so long. As St. Augustine said, "Too late, Oh ancient beauty, have I loved Thee." [211

... Moment Of. The occasion on which the divine thief chooses to steal away our unhappiness may be a moment of satiety with sin, as it was with Leon Bloy, or the sight of death, as it was with St. Francis, or the closeness of the stars and the desert, as it was with Ernest Psichari, or the reading of a book, as it was with Jacques Maritain, or the sound of church bells, as it was with Paul Claudel. Whatever the external circumstances, they are of no importance; they are the occasions on which one individual has met God—but God can be met anywhere. [212

... Sin; Guilt. Those who hold the opinion that the only guilt is the admission of guilt and that the only sin is the belief in sin render themselves incapable of conversion. [213

... Understanding. The best man to convert a drunkard is a converted drunkard. Power to appreciate temptation is the first condition of being able to help others out of temptation. The first step God took toward making us become like Him was to become, as far as He could, like us.   [214

COURAGE

... **Acceptance of God.** It requires more courage than brains to learn to know God: God is the most obvious fact of human experience, but accepting Him is one of the most arduous.   [215

COURTESY

Courtesy in its roots is saintliness; that is why sometimes one will find it in the most unlettered and uneducated. [216

CREATION

Why did God make the universe? . . . God is Good, and being Good He could not, as it were, contain Himself; consequently, He told the secret of His Goodness to nothingness and that was Creation. The world is the overflow of Divine Goodness. Begotten of the Goodness of God, the Goodness of God is in it.   [217

... **Creating.** In creating there is no addition made to the infinity of God's Being, because it is not in the same order as the Being of God. Being in an inferior is possible, because of the analogy of *being*. Nor is there any more being in the world after creation than before. Suppose that there was only one man in the world who had knowledge. Knowledge would be quantitatively and qualitatively one in such a case. Now suppose that learned man should teach a populated world. What would be the result? Knowledge would increase quantitatively; instead of there being one man who knows, there would be millions. But qualitatively the knowledge would remain the same. There would be no more knowledge qualitatively in the world than before . . . This comparison is feeble, but it helps to illustrate the point in question. Creation is an increase of being *extensively* but not *intensively*. There are more beings in the world after creation than before, but there is no more *being;* there are more good things, but the good is not multiplied. Creation introduced the word "have" into the world to denote participation. Before creation there was no such thing as "having"; there was only *being*.   [218

CRIME

... **Education.** The United States is today spending $1.90 on crime for every $1 that it spends on education.
                                                                [219

... **Law.** Unless there is some sharp and fast law to resist the psychological and economic descriptions of crime, it will not be long until a wrong thing will be called a right thing if it is done in a nice manner. The moment is not far off when dramatists, authors and even murderers will describe the taking of human life as the "perfect crime." This is like describing leprosy as the "perfect disease."   [220

CRISIS

... **Character.** Crisis does not create character; it reveals it. Woodsmen say that when a log is thrown into the fire, it reveals all the colors that went into it—the black of the night, the purple of the morning, the red of the sunset, the silver of the stars. In like manner, in time of crisis people reveal what is already in them: the deep love of virtue on the one hand, or their secret lusts on the other.   [221

... **Men; Women.** Which stands up better in a crisis—man or woman? One can discuss this in a series of historical crises, but without arriving at any decision. The best way to arrive at a conclusion is to go to the greatest crisis the world ever faced, namely, the Crucifixion of Our Divine Lord. When we come to this great drama of Calvary, there is one fact that stands out very clearly: men failed . . . On the other hand, there is not a single instance of a woman's failing Him.   [222

CRITICISM

Encouragement is often a better stimulus to improve efforts than any criticism . . . Unhappy lives are already so filled with self-disgust that criticism only deepens their despair. We already have enough critics; now our poor world needs apostles of encouragement. But whence shall they come except from Hope born of a Loving and Merciful Savior?   [223

... **Slander; Jealousy.** The basis of all criticism of neighbor, the source of false judgments, slander, jealousies and pulling down the reputation of others is our refusal to look into our own soul.   [224

CROSS

... **Crucifixion.** The Cross is not something that *has* happened; the Crucifixion is something that *is* happening. It can be found at any place and at any hour in the human

race, for it is the epic struggle of the forces of good and evil.
[225

... **Meaning.** The Cross of Christ does something for us that we cannot do for ourselves. Everywhere else in the world we are spectators; but, facing the vision of the Cross, we pass from spectatorship to participation. If anyone thinks that the confession of his guilt is escapism, let him try once kneeling at the foot of the Crucifix. He cannot escape feeling involved. One look at Christ on the Cross, and the scab is torn from the ulcerous depths of sin as it stands revealed in all of its ugliness. Just one flash of that Light of the World shatters all the blindness which sins have begotten and burns into the soul the truth of our relationship to God.
[226

... **Sinners.** On the Cross He poured forth His blood, not because bloodshed pleased the Father, but because the sinner deserved to die and He, willing to be one with sinners, chose to bear the punishment our sins deserved. [227

... **Way Of.** The Cross is laid on the shoulders of our pride and envy, our lusts and our angers, until by its friction it wears them away, and thus brings us to the great abiding joys of life. [228

CRUCIFIXION

On this particular day, the centurion was executing what to him appeared as just another batch of criminals . . . But when the Man on the central Cross said as the nails pierced

His Hands, "Father, forgive them, for they know not what they do"; when the centurion noticed the absence of all that was bitter and ugly, he began to reflect . . . He could see here that love was conquering hate, and that the One on the Cross was bringing the meaninglessness of hate to naught. For the first time he saw that death could be vicarious and perhaps even suspected the Resurrection as there welled up from his heart the cry: "Indeed this was the Son of God."

[229

There is a personal equation between that Cross and us. Life with its rebellions, its injustices, its sins, all played a role in the Crucifixion. We can no more wash our hands of our guilt than Pilate could wash his as he held them up under a noon-day sun and declared himself innocent.   [230

CRUELTY

. . . Guilt.   The psychological reason for the cruelty in the modern world is this: those who have a deep hidden sense of guilt, feel the need of making some reparation for it. But since they refuse to face their own moral guilt, they inflict on others a punishment which should have been inflicted on themselves.   [231

CULTURE

God does not work through culture but through grace. He does not ask men to be refined; He asks them to be penitent. Thus does God show that we become great not because of what we are, but because of what He gives.   [232

CYNICISM

The cynic who has no God to Whom he can turn in his bitterness is apt to pound himself into suicide, for bitterness does end in self-destruction. [233

Whenever an age or a people become cynical about religion, there is hidden somewhere in souls a bitterness. [234

Cynicism is a screen behind which youth hides its ignorance and old age its sin. [235

· · D · ·

DEATH

There comes a time in the life of every man when at the supreme and tragic hour of death his friends and relatives ask, "How much did he leave?" It is just at that split second God is asking, "How much did he take with him?" It is only the latter question that matters, for it is only our works that follow us. [236

Most men and women are quite unconscious of the injustice, the ingratitude, and the thanklessness of their lives until the cold hand of death is laid upon one they love. It is then, and only then, that they realize (and oh, with what regret!) the haunting poverty of their love and kindness. One of the reasons why the bitterest of tears are shed over graves is because of words left unsaid and deeds left undone. "The child never knew how much I loved her." "He never knew how much he meant to me." [237

... Christ. Every other person who ever came into this world came into it to live. He came into it to die. Death was a stumbling block to Socrates—it interrupted his teaching.

61

But to Christ, death was the goal and fulfillment of His life, the goal that He was seeking.   [238

...**Fear Of.** It is no answer to the fact of death to say that life is like a match which has been struck, which will burn for a moment and then cease to exist. If our life were like a match, death would have no terrors for us, as it has none for animals.   [239

...**Immortality.** The cult of staying young contributes to the macabre pretense that death will never come . . . Modern totalitarianism, with its herd mentality, absorbs persons into a collectivity and leads them to believe that they live in the mass, that they are important only as builders of a better future for the race; individual immortality becomes group immortality—which is no immortality, for even the group, too, will perish in time . . . every man must die before the Utopia he envisions is attained, and the only consolation this philosophy offers him is that his great-grandchildren will dance on his grave.   [240

...**Insensitiveness To.** The modern man seeks to forget about death altogether or—if he cannot do that—to conceal it, to render it unobtrusive, to disguise it. He feels awkward in the presence of death, does not know how to console or what to say . . . For he regards all discussion of death as morbid; yet he will laugh at a comedy in which a dozen people are killed and will stay awake half the night reading a detective story about a murder. This, too, is *death,* and it enthralls him; but he concentrates upon the circumstances by which death comes, rather than upon the eternal issues of

62

death, which alone are all-important. This modern insensitiveness to death is an insensitiveness to personality, to the moral order, and to destiny. [241

... Meaningfulness. All men share a profound intuition that their deaths can serve a triumphant purpose. Why is a man less willing to die in a train wreck or an automobile accident than he is to be killed on a battlefield or as a martyr to his faith? Is it not because death is less terrifying and more meaningful as soon as we rise above the level of the commonplace and lift ourselves into the realm of eternal values where, alone, death has meaning? [242

... Morticians. Today's morticians make death look like life; they pretend that all that it involves is a little sleep, after which everyone will wake up on an eternal shore which has no passport regulations. [243

... Of A Loved One. Tears are shed in vain before eyes which cannot see; caresses are offered without response to arms that cannot embrace, and sighs stir not a heart whose ear is deaf. Oh, then the anguish for not offering the flowers before death had come and for not sprinkling the incense while the beloved was still alive and for not speaking the kind words that now must die on the very air they cleave. Oh, the sorrow at the thought that we cannot atone for the stinted affection we gave them, for the light answers we returned to their pleading, and for the lack of reverence we showed to one who was perhaps the dearest thing that God had ever given us to know. [244

...Preparation. When death is a personal threat, modern man is afraid to look upon its face. Physicians no longer warn their patients of the imminence of death; they act as if there were no preparation needed for eternity. [245

DEBAUCHERY

Debauchery is an effect of personal sin which seeks external expression, in this case by corrupting others. For the inwardly empty cannot bear their burden alone—they tend to empty society of whatever values it possesses. Solitariness of the soul creates its own atmosphere and makes a solitary world. Self-expression, understood as the expression of the animal self whose satisfactions are external, thus begets not only its own destruction but also the dissolution of peaceful society. The traditional restraints and moral sanctions of society come to be regarded more and more as worthless, outworn taboos or as cruel checks placed upon individual egotism, which now goes under the name of freedom. A stage is eventually reached where there is no acknowledged limit to self-expression. The most traitorous deeds are defended as civil rights; the defense of even the natural law is ridiculed as "medieval." This lawlessness, if widespread, creates such confusion in society that a tyrant soon arises to organize the chaos through force. Thus is fulfilled the dictum of Dostoevski that "unlimited freedom leads to unlimited tyranny." [246

DECADENCE

...Values. One of the marks of decadence in society is the exaltation of little insignificant codes at the expense of great and eternal moral principles . . . Dishpan hands in an advertising world are a greater tragedy than dishonest deeds. Codes are multiplied about the necessity of clean paper cups lest lips become polluted, but any censorship of garbage that enters the mind is looked upon as a restriction of freedom. [247

DECLARATION OF INDEPENDENCE

... **Man's Rights And Liberties.** Where do we get our rights and liberties which we have to defend? . . . Our Founding Fathers had to face this question, and it was one of the very first that they answered. They looked around the world for an answer. England was saying that rights and liberties come from Parliament, and the new French school was saying, the rights and liberties of man come from the will of the majority. But our Founding Fathers knew very well that if your rights and liberties of man come from the will of the majority, the will of the majority could take away the rights of the minority . . . So they sought for some basis and ground of human rights and liberties, and they found it and set it down in the second paragraph of the Declaration of Independence: it is a self-evident principle that the Creator—*the Creator*—has endowed man with certain unalienable rights. Unalienable rights. They cannot be taken away. [248

DEGENERACY

Very serious effects follow the abandonment of oneself to biological and animal instincts. It increases despair and morbidity; the individual becomes trapped in the license to which he submits. Freedom is destroyed when the victim becomes a slave to something external. Scripture tells us that he who sins becomes a slave to sin. This kind of self-expression, instead of allowing a person to become self-possessed, ends in his losing control over the self and making it other-possessed, which is the new form of modern slavery.

[249

DEGRADATION

The great Greek historian, Lecky, said that the surest sign of utter degradation is when men speak of virtues as if they were vices, and of vices as if they were virtues.   [250

DEMOCRACY

... **Communism.** Democracy today finds it hard to make up its mind on what is right. Communism, on the contrary, has made up its mind on what is wrong. All its passions are devoted to the evil . . . Leadership in democracies cannot come out of the ashes of spineless indifference. When more get mad, not because they lose money, but because right is ignored and wrong enthroned, then the fires will come back to democracy; fires which will burn like beacons summoning men to a finer and better world.   [251

... **Conformity.** Democracy cannot survive where there is such conformity that everyone wears exactly the same intellectual uniform or point of view.   [252

... **Endowment.** Be not deceived by slogans about Democracy, as if it were like an heirloom, which once possessed needs only to be preserved. Democracy is an endowment like life, and needs to be repurchased in each new generation.

[253

66

. . . God-Given. God said nothing about the necessity of democracy. But He told Pilate what we, 1700 years later, wrote in the Declaration of Independence—that all rights and liberties come from God. [254

. . . Issues. Democracy does not mean that because both sides ought to be heard, there is no right side. [255

. . . Meaning. Democracy worthy of the name can have no other meaning than to place the citizen increasingly in a position to hold his own personal opinion, to express it and even to make it prevail for the common good. [256

DEPENDENCE

Nothing in the universe reaches its perfection without some dependence on or relation to the external. Not even the coal will give light and heat without first a fire being applied to it; even then it releases the energy the sun stored up in it centuries before. The grain of wheat will not send forth the green stalk without contact with the environment of another world than itself. Why then does man think his basic worries, fears and inner unhappiness can be cured by himself and within himself? The best violin and bow in the world will produce no harmonies without an outside hand endowed with talent. [257

DEPRAVITY

As pure water becomes loathsome to the drunkard, so do justice and virtue to the depraved conscience . . . No condition of the mind is worse than to forget the heavens from which we fell, for then we lose all aspirations for conversion. [258

DESIRE

Desire is to the soul what gravitation is to matter. When we know our desires, we know the direction our soul is taking. [259

... **Carnal.** Our Blessed Lord never said that carnal desires in themselves were evil. He said only that we must not permit them to burden the soul with such anxiety for their satisfaction that we lose the greater treasures. [260

... **For God.** The natural tendency of the intellect toward truth and of the will toward love would alone signify that there is in man a natural desire for God. There is not a single striving or pursuit or yearning of the human heart, even in the midst of the most sensual pleasures, that is not a dim grasping after the Infinite. As the stomach yearns for food and the eye for light and the ear for harmony, so the soul craves God. [261

... **Satisfaction.** The modern world is geared to increase our desires and our wants by its advertising, but it can never satisfy them. Our desires are infinite; the supply of any good on earth is finite. Hence our unhappiness and anxieties, our disappointments and our sadness. [262

DESPAIR

If man were like an ant, a creature only of this world, he would never despair; it takes eternity to make a man despair. [263

... **Eternity.** Cows have no psychoses, and pigs have no neuroses, and chickens are not frustrated (unless these frustrations are artificially produced by man); neither would man be frustrated or have an anxiety complex if he were an animal made only for this world. [264

... **Misery.** To be conscious of one's misery as so many are in the modern world, and yet not to know the mercy of the Heavenly Father, is to despair. [265

... **Unrepented Sin.** The condition of despair induced by unrepented sin often reaches a point where there is a positive fanaticism against religion and morality. He who has fallen away from the spiritual order will hate it, because religion is the reminder of his guilt. [266

DESPOTISM
... **Socialism.** History shows no instance of people with well-distributed property suffering from despotism. But a close relationship exists between despotism and socialism . . . where private property is not allowed, in that land there is no political or economic freedom. [267

DESTINY
... **Dread.** Modern man is uncertain of his destiny. He is always afraid of being thrown back into the nothingness from which he came . . . The result is dread. Much of modern culture is directed to the suppression of that dread: sleeping tablets, opiates, constant search for pleasures—all these are attempts to suppress this awful, gnawing dread of nothingness. [268

DEVIL
Though contemporary atheism has not convinced us there is no God, it has convinced us that there is a devil. [269

69

Today there is a general tendency to deny the existence of the devil, and never is he so powerful as when men say he does not exist . . . Does the devil insinuate himself into the church? . . . The devil is in our church when he tells us "Build up your parish halls and forget the other parishes of the world. Increase your surpluses and ignore the poor bishops in Latin America who have four priests to cover parishes of 100,000 square miles. Do not sacrifice to bring Christ to lands other than America . . ." [270

. . . Description. Nowhere in Sacred Scripture do we find warrant for the popular myth of the Devil as a buffoon . . . Rather is he described as an angel fallen from heaven, and as "the Prince of this world," whose business is to tell us that there is no other world. [271

DIFFICULTY
. . . Love. If one loves, everything is easy; if one does not—everything is hard. [272

DIGNITY
. . . Degradation. It is possible that Flaubert was right when he said, "As humanity perfects itself, man begins to lose his dignity." [273

DISBELIEF
Disbelief is born of sin, not of reason. [274

DISCIPLINE
. . . Lack Of. There is nothing so destructive of personality as a want of discipline. [275

... **Love.** Obedience is easy when dictated by love, or better, inspired by it. The more respect there is for the one who gives the command, the easier it is to comply. Where there is little respect, obedience is difficult . . . Parents, therefore, are not to be like a herder with a stick and a dog who herds the cattle to market, but rather as a shepherd going before his sheep lovingly leading the way.   [276

... **Moral Force.** Moral force is like running water in a narrow channel. It rushes forward to the field where it is to dispense fertility, but it must have barriers to confine its energies and direct its course. The difference between a swamp and a river is that the swamp has no bank. The parent who is guided by emotion is a swamp.   [277

. . . **Obedience.** Civilization is always in danger when those who have never learned to obey are given the right to command.   [278

DISCORD

Let those who call themselves Catholics, or Protestant, or Jews recall that the function of their religion is to intensify the spiritual life of man and not to empty the vials of bitterness into hearts, stirring up one against another.   [279

DISEASE

... **Cancer.** One wonders if civilization does not have, at various times in history, certain diseases which are symptomatic and symbolic of the spiritual ills of sin. If this be so, cancer is perhaps the symbol of our civilization in the sense that it is a mask. It often claims the victim before he is conscious of its seriousness. There is also a peculiar psychological effect associated with it, namely, the tendency to deny or ignore its existence; even doctors are unwilling to tell their patients of the seriousness of it, thereby denying them an opportunity to make their peace with God before they die.

[280

DISORDER

... **Man; Self-Control.** The totalitarian regimes are symptomatic of a disease which has also attacked the men and women in countries that are free. It is the disease of disorder within man. Few realize the terrible dimensions of the present catastrophe; they are blinded by the fact that man has made great material progress. The truth of the matter is, however, that man has lost control over himself at the very moment when he has gained control over nature. Because man has lost self-control and denied the spiritual purpose in life, he utilizes for destructive ends the forces of nature which he has harnessed. The atomic bomb is a perfect symbol of the disintegration of the modern personality. Every gain in mastery of the forces of nature becomes a potential danger unless it is matched by an equal gain in man's mastery over his animal impulses.   [281

DIVINE ACTION

Divine action on the soul is internal and is so incommunicably personal that the man may sometimes feel that it is his own creation. The impact of God on the soul is not that of a proselytist, for a proselytist works from without, like one billiard ball upon another. But God, although working through His Apostles, allows their words to affect the soul

from within by "immanent activity," which is the characteristic method by which living things grow.   [282

DIVINE LIFE

As the sun rises without asking permission of the night, so
Divine life invades us without consulting the darkness of our
minds. God establishes His beachhead in our most unsus-
pecting moments, almost in secret, without our being consciously aware of Him. He comes as a sudden thought that
springs into the mind, an intense desire that moves the will.
His entrance is imperceptible; in the beginning, we do not
know that it is He. We do not resist Him, for we have no
sense of an alien interference. We may even think that the
sudden upsurge of our spirit is our own, with no suspicion
that it comes from God—just as we may think that our eyes
do all the seeing, without being conscious of their reliance on
the sun. It is only later that we understand, looking back,
that the initiative was divine and eternal.   [283

DIVINE LOVE

All the popular love songs tell us: "How happy we will
be!" Divine love, on the contrary, does not look at all en-
chanting or ecstatic before we have it: the Cross frightens
us; the sacrifice of selfishness and sin seems like a little
death, nonsensual love appears as lovelessness. But after one
makes the surrender, gives up the field to win the pearl, then
one is possessed of a joy that is ineffable, that beggars all
description. The discovery makes one act so differently that
his friends think he has lost his mind; but actually, he has
found his soul, which the believer would not now give up
for anything in all the world.   [284

73

DIVORCE

... **Christ; Cross.** The tragedy of our times is divorce in all of its works and pomps. The greatest of all divorces is that of Christ from His cross. The Western world has divorced Christ from His Cross while Communism takes up the Cross and, therefore, has the Cross without Christ. [285

DOCTRINE

... **Method.** The distinction between method and doctrine must be rigidly preserved. A scientist may study things through a yellow glass: that is his method of working. But if he concludes that everything is yellow, he has enunciated a doctrine. [286

DOGMA

To say we want no dogmas in religion is to assert a dogma. [287

DREAD

Dread is related to an unknown, overwhelming, all-powerful something—which may strike one knows not when or where. Dread is everywhere and nowhere, all around us, terrible and indefinite, threatening man with an annihilation which he cannot imagine or even conceive. Such fear is man's alone. Because an animal has no soul capable of knowing perfect love, because it has to render no account of its stewardship beyond the corridors of the grave, because it is not like a pendulum swinging between eternity and time, it is devoid of those eternal relationships which man possesses; therefore it can have only a sick body, never a sick soul. Thus a psychology which denies the human soul is constantly contradicting itself. It calls man an animal and then proceeds to describe a human anxiety which is never found in any animal devoid of a rational soul. [288

DRUNKARDS

... Alcoholics.   A drunkard could stop drinking if he wanted to; an alcoholic may not want to get drunk, but he is overwhelmed by an irresistible impulse. The drunkard is what he is because of wrong choices at the present moment; the alcoholic is what he is because of wrong choices in the past. [289

DUTIES

The smallest duties are often harder, because of their apparent insignificance and their constant recurrence. [290

·· E ··

EASTER

The law He gave was clear: life is a struggle; unless there is a Cross in our lives, there will never be an empty tomb; unless there is the crown of thorns, there will never be the halo of light; unless there is a Good Friday, there will never be an Easter Sunday.   [291

The Divine Savior never said to His Apostles: "Be good and you will not suffer;" but He did say: "In this world you shall have tribulations." He told them not to fear those that kill the body, but rather to fear those who can kill the soul . . . He told the Apostles that His life was a model for all of His followers . . . It was the Cross of Christ that raised the questions of life; it was the Resurrection that answered them.   [292

It is not His Sermon on the Mount that He would have us remember, but His Cross. There would have been no gospel had there been no Cross; and the death on the Cross would have been useless for the removal of human guilt, if He had not risen from the dead. He said it behooved Him to suffer because He had to show the evil of sin, and evil is most manifest in the Crucifixion of Goodness . . . Having been defeated in that, it could never be victorious again.   [293

After the women had gone to notify the Apostles, the guards, who had been standing about the tomb, and who were witnesses to the Resurrection, came into the city of Jerusalem and told the chief priests all that had been done. The chief priests immediately assembled a meeting of the Sanhedrin, the express purpose of which was to bribe the guards . . . they would buy a lie to escape the purifying Blood of the Lamb. The bribery of the guard was really a stupid way to escape the face of the Resurrection. First of all, there was the problem of what would be done with His Body after the disciples had possession of it. All that the enemies of our Lord would have had to do to disprove the Resurrection would be to produce the Body. Quite apart from the fact that it was very unlikely that a whole guard of Roman soldiers slept while they were on duty, it was absurd for them to say that what had happened, happened when they were asleep. The soldiers were advised to say they were asleep; and yet they were so awake as to have seen thieves and to know that they were disciples. If all of the soldiers were asleep, they could never have discovered the thieves; if a few of them were awake, they should have prevented the theft. It is equally improbable that a few timid disciples should attempt to steal their Master's Body from a grave closed by stone, officially sealed, and guarded by soldiers without awakening the sleeping guards . . . The crime was certainly greater in the bribers than in the bribed; for the council was educated and religious; the soldiers were untutored and simple. The Resurrection of Christ was officially

77

proclaimed to the civil authorities; the Sanhedrin believed
in the Resurrection before the Apostles.   [294

. . . Giving. Your gratitude for the first Easter Sunday can
be shown this Easter by your compassion for Christ, still
suffering in His Mystical body—in the world's starving and
diseased. Christ gave His life for us. What more worthy gift
can we give to Christ than our life-work?   [295

. . . Women. It was to a virgin woman that the birth of
the Son of God was announced. It was to a fallen woman
that His Resurrection was announced.   [296

. . . Resurrection. The Cross has asked the question:
Why does God permit evil and sin to nail Justice to the tree?
The Resurrection answers; that sin, having done its worst,
exhausts itself. Sin is thus overcome by Love, which is
stronger even than sin or death.   [297

. . . Victory. Victory is complete when Love conquers
hate and death and rises to the new Life on Easter.   [298

ECONOMICS

. . . Communism. Economics has gone to the head of the
Communists like wine to an empty stomach.   [299

. . . Modern. Certain natives of Australia do not know
how to count above 3. They say, "1, 2, 3. Enough." Their
philosophy of economics puts a limit on externals, and probably makes them more carefree than we who count by bil-
lions.   [300

ECUMENISM

We may not be able to meet in the same pew—would to God we did—but we can meet on our knees.   [301

EDUCATION

Too often, teaching is really nothing else than the communication of information from the note book of a professor to the note book of a student, without passing through the mind of either.   [302

... **American Heritage.** If education is to guard our American heritage it must ever keep in mind the meaning and purpose of life, namely, that we were really made for God as well as for this earth.   [303

... **Children.** An educator was once asked by a mother of a child of five years of age, at what age she should begin educating her child. His answer was that 'it is already five years too late.' This may be an exaggeration, but the best informed opinions are that the two ages which are most important in the education of the young are the ages between three and four for psychological development, and the beginning of the 'teens' for ethical development.   [304

... **Ignorance.** There is apt to be the assumption of Socrates in education that the only reason people are bad is because they are ignorant, and if you give them enough education, they will be good. Oh, no. Sometimes education can make clever devils instead of stupid devils. Not every Ph.D is a saint, nor every D.D. I am both, and I am not a saint.   [305

...Leisure. Our education is rightly preparing us to make a living. But let education not forget that since man has more leisure than working hours, it might teach him how to spend his leisure. [306

...Men; Women. Education today makes no difference between the training of man and woman. This is right from the point of view of opportunities that are open to both; but it is short-sighted when one considers the psychological differences between the two. [307

...Philosophy. A little child who today is telling a Sister in school that God made him, that he was made to know, love, and serve God, and to be happy with Him in the next world, knows more, and is more profoundly educated, than all the professors throughout the length and breadth of this land who babble about spacetime deities, who prattle about new ethics to fit unethical lives, who negate all morality to suit their unmoral thinking, but who do not know, therefore, that beyond time is the timeless, beyond space is the spaceless, the Infinite Lord and Master of the Universe. [308

...Purpose. The purpose of education is not merely to train for a democracy. That we must do, but that cannot be the final end. The purpose of education cannot merely mean to earn our economic living. The purpose of education is the training of the whole man, body and soul. [309

...Religious Schools. In the beginning of our national life practically all of our schools and colleges were religious schools. It was assumed by our Constitution and by its spirit that they would be religious. The reason was obvious. If human dignity and liberty come from God, then it follows that loss of faith in Him means loss of faith in those liberties which derive from Him. [310

... Truth. Modern education is geared to what it calls "extending the frontiers of truth," and sometimes this ideal is prized and used to excuse men from acting on old truths already discovered. The discovery of the size of a distant star creates no moral obligation; but the old truths about the nature and destiny of man can be a reproach to the way one lives. [311

EDUCATORS
... Authority. Very often those educators who boast of being opposed to all authority are themselves the ones who bow down profoundly before that anonymous authority "they." For example, "They are wearing green this year," or "They say that belief in God is medieval." [312

EGO
... Atheism. The modern god can be the ego, or self. This is atheism. [313

EGOTISM
Hell is composed of completely egotistic persons! . . . In hell, nothing burns but the ego—a sensation that egotists dimly feel in the gnawing that goes on inside their conscience . . . Paradoxical as it may seem, happiness begins when the ego dies. [314

...**Psychosis.** Practically every psychotic person is an egotist. [315

ELEVATION

...**Sublimation.** The great problem, facing every human, concerns, not sublimation, but elevation. Is he willing to surrender the lower to find the ecstasies of the higher? Does he want God enough to overcome the obstacles that keep Him away? Does he love the sunlight enough to open the blinds his own agnosticism has drawn down? [316

EMPLOYMENT

...**Investment.** The investment of large income in such a manner that favorable opportunity for employment may abound, is to be considered an act of real liberality, particularly appropriate to the needs of our times. If, therefore, a man accumulates a vast fortune, he is acting within the bounds of justice if he turns back some of that money into his business, in order to increase the common good, to give men work, and to further the prosperity of his country. [317

...**Russia.** In the Soviet Constitution . . . Article 131 regards all strikers as "enemies of the people." The Communists tell our American workers that they are working for exploiters. Maybe a few are, but employers are not all exploiters. Even if they were, at least in the United States a man can go from one exploiter to another. But when the state is the only exploiter, as in Russia, you can go nowhere else, except to Siberia. [318

EMPTINESS

...**Man.** In our emptiness we are really looking to Him to fill us. We may deny the water, but we may never

deny the thirst; we may deny God, but we are seeking Him
even in our denial.   [319

ENEMIES

... **Hatred.** Our enemy is often our savior; our persecu-
tor is often our redeemer; our executioners are often our
allies; our crucifiers are often our benefactors—for they reveal what is selfish, base, conceited and ignoble in us. But we
must not hate them for that. To hate them for hating us is
weakness.   [320

... **Love.** If you have enemies, if they hate you, if they
revile you, and persecute and say all manner of evil things
against you, and you wish to stop their hatred, to release the
hatred in their clenched fists, drive them off the face of the
earth—there is but one way to do it—Love them!   [321

ENERGY

Hell is full of the talented, but Heaven, of the energetic.
                                                          [322

ENVIRONMENT

The cause of conflict is not environment, because the
golden bit does not make the better horse. Judas, who had
the best environment in history, died in ignominy and
shame.   [323

... **Responsibility.** Hardly anyone today challenges the
view that character is made by outside or external influences,
such as his home background, his schooling, his poverty or
wealth, the propaganda to which he was subjected and the
neighborhood in which he was raised. This view could lead

83

to the destruction of responsibility if carried to extremes; and responsibility, it must not be forgotten, is the mark of freedom.   [324

ENVY

Some believe that the good qualities of others have been stolen from them.   [325

EQUALITY

... **Faith.** In vain will the world seek for equality until it has seen men through the eyes of faith. Faith teaches that all men, however poor or ignorant or crippled, however maimed or ugly or degraded they may be, all bear within themselves the image of God, and have been bought by the precious blood of Jesus Christ. As this truth is forgotten, men are valued only because of what they can do, not because of what they *are*.   [326

ESCAPISM

... **Escapists.** Escapists refuse to face the fact that their own lives are disordered; or else they try an "easy" way out of their misery which lands them in confusion worse confounded. Some of the "easy" ways out are the escapism of scandal-mongering, which seeks to find others who are worse than the self and thus make the self seem good by comparison; the escapism of ridicule, which makes fun of the virtuous and religious to avoid the reproach of their goodness; the escapism of noise, of drowning oneself in excitement, crowds, collective trances, so that the sweet, low voice of conscience, through which God speaks, is never heard.   [327

... **Guilt.** A man cannot escape what he is flying from. Guilt pursues him almost like a shadow. He reaches a point where he is no longer a bad man but an evil man. A bad man will do wrong things, such things as cheat, steal, slander, murder, and violate, but he will still admit the law ... An evil man, on the contrary, may not do any of these bad things; he is concerned not with the concrete but with the abstract. His desire is to completely destroy goodness, religion, morality in a mad bigotry.   [328

ETERNITY

... **Yearning.** Our hunger for the infinite is never quieted; even those disillusioned by excess of pleasures have always kept in their imagination a hope of somewhere finding a truer source of satisfaction than any they have tried. Our search for the never-ending love is never ended—no one could really love anything unless he thought of it as eternal. Not everyone gives a name to this infinity toward which he tends and for which he yearns, but it is what the rest of us call God.   [329

EVIL

The evil of our day is not of the East or of the West, but of the world.   [330

... **Effects.** The evil which God permits must not be judged by its immediate effects, but rather by its ultimate effects. When you go to a theatre, you do not walk out because you see a good man suffering in the first act. You give the dramatist credit for a plot. Why can not you do that much with God?   [331

...Freedom. The evil of the world is inseparable from human freedom, and hence the cost of destroying the world's evil would be the destruction of human freedom.   [332

...Love. Evil is never rooted up; it languishes for want of love.   [333

EVOLUTION

Evolution from the original gas or molecule would demand three things: a Power which brought that gas or molecule into being, and which sustains it in being during its progressive unfolding; a Mind which planned the evolution of that primary matter and endowed it with internal laws; a Will which chose to bring it into being, impressed each emergent of that evolutionary process with its inner finality, and gave to the whole process its own goal and purpose—for without some purpose there would be no reason for ever evolving.   [334

...God. What is evolution but the immanence of God expressed in dynamic terms?   [335

...Grace. One wonders why a world so much given to the philosophy of evolution does not see the grace of Jesus Christ as the answer to its aspirations. One of the reasons why evolution is held so highly is because of the promise it gives for the future, and yet, all that it can give, even in its wildest form, is the unfolding of something beneath man. But here in supernatural biology, there is the promise and the potency of a glory for man which exceeds even his imagination—the potency not of becoming a superman, but

86

a son of God. There is no emergent in the whole field of evolution comparable to the "new creatures" which emerge from the Sacrament of Baptism.   [336

EXPLANATION

... **Description.** There is a certain type of mentality which confuses description with explanation, and feels that because we are now learning the law of things, therefore they could not possibly be made by God.   [337

· · F · ·

FAITH

...**Acceptance.** The things that happen to us are not always susceptible to our minds' comprehension or wills' conquering; but they are always within the capacity of our faith to accept and of our wills' submission.   [338

...**Belief.** Faith in religion is like credit in business; before a store will extend credit to a person, there must be an investigation; only when there are reasonable grounds for extending credit is it ever given. So with faith; there must be reasonable motives for believing before there is belief . . . Faith has nothing, absolutely nothing to do with the emotions. Those who when asked why they believe something, sometimes answer: "I felt it down here" are equivalently identifying faith with a full stomach or a glandular reaction.   [339

...**Gift Of God.** You cannot argue, or study, or reason, or hypnotize, or whip yourself, into faith. Faith is a gift of God. When anyone instructs you in Christian doctrine, he does not give you faith. He is only a spiritual agriculturist, tilling the soil of your soul, uprooting a few weeds and

88

breaking up the clods of egotism. It is God who drops the seed. "For by grace you are saved through faith, and that not of yourselves, for it is the gift of God."   [340

...**Loss of Belief.** Have you not noticed that as a man ceases to believe in God, he also ceases to believe in man? Have you observed that, if you have worked for or with a person of deep faith in Christ, you have always been treated with gentleness, equality, and charity. You could not point to a single person who truly loves God and is mean to his fellowman. Have you noticed that as men lose faith in God, they become selfish, immoral, and cruel? On a cosmic scale, as religion decreases, tyranny increases; as men lose faith in Divinity, they lose faith in humanity. Where God is outlawed, there man is subjugated.   [341

...**Nature Of.** The nature of the act of faith was revealed by Our Lord's attitude toward the unbelieving Pharisees. They had seen miracles worked and prophecies fulfilled. They were not lacking in motives for belief. But they still refused to believe. Our Lord took a little child in His midst and said: "Amen I say to you, whosoever shall not receive the kingdom of God as a little child, shall not enter into it."   [342

...**Reason.** Faith is not a dam which prevents the flow of the river of reason and thought; it is a levee which prevents unreason from flooding the countryside.   [343

...**Reason.** In other religions, doubts increase with the development of reason, but in the Church faith intensifies as reason develops.   [344

89

... Result Of. As a stained glass window looks different from the inside of the church from what it does from the outside, so all the great problems of life take on a new meaning and significance when one takes his stand inside the Faith. [345

FAITHFULNESS

... Character. Faithfulness in great things is not uncommon; faithfulness in little things is rare but most indicative of true character. [346

FALSE GODS

No false gods who are immune from pain and sorrow can solace us in these tragic days. No false deities who never felt the traitor's kiss or the blow of injustice can give us any assurance of hope. Only the Son of the Living God Who arose from the dead can assure us of the eventual triumph of good over evil. [347

FAMILIES

... Large; Small. There is generally less selfishness in large families than in small. [348

FATALISM

We are not to be like the man who perilously walked the railing of a ship in a storm at sea saying: "I am a fatalist! I believe that when your time comes, there is nothing you can do about it." There was much more wisdom in the preacher who said: "You run up against a brick wall every now and then during life. If God wants you to go through that wall, it is up to God to make the hole." [349

FATIGUE

...Mental. Mental fatigue is due to worry. Many people are tired in body because they are already tired in mind. Interested spectators at a football game are much more exhausted at the end of the game than the players.   [350

FAULTS

We often carry our faults in sacks behind our backs and the faults of our neighbors in open baskets in front of us.
[351

...Neighbors. Most of us know our neighbors better than we know ourselves. We can tell all their faults, enumerate all the scandals about them and even add a few for good measure, but we are hardly conscious of any single fault of our own.   [352

FEAR

If we only knew it, we are fearing the wrong things. We used to fear God; now we fear our fellow man.   [353

...Anxieties. The difference between normal fears and anxieties is this: Normal fears are physical. Abnormal fears or anxieties are psychical or mental. Normal fears derive from an *object* external to us, such as an explosion or a tiger. Abnormal fears or anxieties come from the *subject,* that is, our inner self. It is normal to fear what may happen on the outside. The abnormal anxiety—and this is a very modern one—is fear because of something that happens inside of us.
[354

...God's Love. Most souls are afraid of God precisely because of His Goodness.   [355

...God's Love. Our greatest fear is not that God may not love us enough but that He may love us too much. [356

...Love. What are worry and fear, which so much concern our modern world? Fear actually is related to love, as are all passions. Fear is the emotion that rises in us when there is a danger facing something or someone that we love, e.g., our good name, our children, our fortune. The catalogue of fears is the catalogue of loves. Love is attraction for an object; fear is flight from it.   [357

...Servile; Filial. Servile fear is the fear of punishment, such as citizens have for a cruel dictator. Filial fear is the fear of hurting someone we love. A child disobeys his mother; he may do one of two things. He may say, "Mommy, I am sorry I did wrong. Now I can't go to the movies, can I?" That is servile fear. He might also throw his arms around the mother's neck and say, "Mommy, I am sorry I hurt you." That is filial fear.   [358

FEMININITY

...Motherhood. The essence of femininity is readiness to be a mother, either physically or spiritually. A woman becomes a mother physically by the creation of new life, spiritually by the caring for it in the social or spiritual realm.   [359

FLATTERY

The amount of flattery one spreads on another depends on either how much one wishes to exalt his own ego, or how much one wishes to deceive the ego of the hearer . . . A Bishop who was just consecrated was laughingly told, "from now on you will never hear the truth again." [360

FORGIVENESS

As a tree will sometimes bathe with perfume the axe that cuts it, so He let fall from His lips for the first time in the hearing of men the words, "Father forgive them; they know not what they do." "Forgive them"—the neighbors, everybody, you and me. Forgive—Why? "Because they know not what they do." When someone else does us wrong, we say, "He should have known better." Yet He, with His Divine Wisdom, said, "They do not know what they do." [361

. . . **Forgiving Others.** We must forgive others for on no other condition will our own sins be forgiven. In fact, it is almost a moral impossibility for God to forgive us unless we in turn forgive. Has He not said: "Blessed are the merciful: for they shall obtain mercy" . . . "Forgive, and you shall be forgiven. Give, and it shall be given unto you . . . For with the same measure that you shall mete withal, it shall be measured to you again." [362

. . . **Redemption.** The hardened heart may relax its defenses against God at any stage, early or late, and He will enter it. The thief who cursed and blasphemed Our Lord on the Cross was the same thief who, a few moments later, asked to be remembered, and to him came the quick assurance of the Saviour: "This day thou shalt be with me in Paradise." [363

FREEDOM

... License. A long time ago, long before Oedipus and Electra, God wrote a beautiful symphony of creation; chemicals, flowers, and animals were subject to man, man's passions were under the guidance of reason, and man's personality was in love with Love, which is God. God gave that symphony to man and woman to play, with a complete set of directions, down to the last detail of what to avoid. Man and woman, being free, could obey the divine director and produce harmony, or they could disobey Him. The devil suggested that, because the divine director had marked the script and told them what to play and what not to play, He was destroying their freedom. The woman first succumbed to the idea that freedom is license, or absence of law; she struck a discord to prove her so-called "independence." It was a very unladylike thing to do. She then induced man to do the same—which was a very ungentlemanly thing to do. On and on through the whole human race this original discord swept; whenever there was the conjunction of man and woman, it affected every human being, save one, who ever was born, for each inherited the effects of that disharmony. [364

... Moral. If freedom is the right to do whatever you please then freedom is not moral, but physical. [365

FREEDOM OF CHOICE

The power is there to make us different than we are; it is for our freedom to decide if we will respond, and if we are willing to pay the price of having the dross burned off the gold in the flames of love. Let it not be said by anyone, "I am too foul; I am a beast; I am not worthy to be lifted up." It was to assure just such persons as these that He was born in a stable, and on His first night in this world companioned with beasts. [366

Nature gives man corn but he must grind it; God gives man a will, but he must make the right choices. [367

FREEDOM OF SPEECH

Too many of our citizens think of freedom only as the right to make a speech. [368

A Communist who uses freedom of speech to destroy freedom of speech has used the vehicle of words for an evil purpose, and is to be judged in exactly the same way as a motorist who uses his car to run down pedestrians. [369

FREEDOM OF WILL

In a certain sense, even God took a great risk when He made man free, for the very freedom to become a Son of the Eternal Father implied the possibility of becoming a rebel . . . Is it any impeachment of God that He did not care to reign over an empire of stones? [370

FREE WILL

No amount of libido, or passion, no external force, and no inner prompting to sin can make the human action of man anything but free. We are never tempted beyond our strength. Every moral failure is ours alone, because our choices are our own. [371

FREUD

... Freudianism. Whatever be the primary reasons for the present overemphasis on sex, it must not be attributed to Freud himself. A distinction must in fairness be made between Freud and Freudianism, a kind of pan-Sexism which reduces everything to sex in a way that Freud himself never intended. [372

FRIENDSHIP

The best friends are those who know how to keep the same silences. [373

FRUSTRATION

It is an interesting psychological fact that the frustrated soul hates goodness and wants to be separated from it. Every sinner hides from God. [374

... Causes. Man becomes frustrated by having no over-all purpose in life but only multiple desires; by the pursuit of popularity as the essence of happiness; by making the end of life the acquisition of power, either economic or political; by converging all human activities in expression of the subhuman and the erotic. (This is one of the principle sources of frustration because it sets in opposition the body and the soul.) Man also becomes frustrated by making the goal of his life the search for truth while denying either its existence or its absoluteness. [375

... Individuals; Society. It often happens that an individual who is frustrated may look for some kind of escape in sexual promiscuity. So it is with society. [376

FUTURISM

... Humanism. The futurism of the humanistic views of history gives no value to the individuals who live at the present time or to the individuals who have lived in the past, except as instruments to a future happiness in an indefinite future. It is an outrageous affront for persons who are ends in themselves, to be told they are in reality only sticks to be thrown into a great cosmic bonfire to keep it blazing for a generation yet to be born. [377

· · G · ·

GAMBLERS

A professional gambler is one who is unconsciously afraid of the responsibilities of life and particularly poverty.   [378

GIVING

... **Love.** Giving alone does not prove love; but love must manifest itself in giving.   [379

GOALS

... **Christian.** The Christian has fixed his goal, namely, to make his life more and more Christ-like. His own nature is like a block of marble, and his will is the chisel. He looks out upon his model, Christ, and with the sharp points of his mortifying chisel, cuts away from his nature great huge chunks of cold selfishness, and then by finer and more delicate touches makes the great model appear forthwith, until finally only the brush of a hand is needed to give it its polished finish.   [380

... **Necessity.** Men who live in this moral twilight between faith and lack of faith have rarely a clear notion of the purpose of life. Yet a man must have a goal before he can live.   [381

GOD

... Communists. The Communists do not deny God; they merely challenge God. They are not like college sophomores who deny God because they have read the first ten pages of a biology textbook . . . they are fighting against Him because they know He exists. Someday they will love Him.   [382

... Exile Of. The exile of God always means the tyrannization of man.   [383

... Favoritism. God does not show Himself equally to all creatures. He does show all men how to turn everything to joy. This does not mean God is unfair, but only that it is impossible for even Him to show Himself to certain hearts under some conditions. The sunlight has no favorites, but it cannot shine as well on a dusty mirror as on a polished one.   [384

... Fear of. Adam had no fear of God before he disobeyed. After his sin, God seemed to be an angry God. To the bad conscience God appears always the God of wrath . . . Anger is not in God; anger is in our disordered selves.   [385

... Man. God will not fail; it is only our human desire that is weak.   [386

... Man. God, Who became Man, preexisted His Own Mother, as an artist preexists his own painting.   [387

. . . Man. A man without God is not like a cake without raisins; he is like the cake without the flour and milk; he lacks the essential ingredients of happiness. [388

. . . Man. God does not love us because we are lovely or loveable; His love exists not on account of our character, but on account of His. [389

. . . Man's Value. God does not love us because we are valuable; we are valuable because He loves us. [390

. . . Shouting. Why is God never represented as shouting in Revealed Scripture or in the writings of any religious people? It is because He is so near He has no need to shout. [391

. . . Truth; Love. God acts in the intellect as truth, and in the will as love. He sometimes strikes the soul with a terrific mystical impact which demands a complete break with everything external. [392

THE "GOD IS DEAD" MOVEMENT

One day, when out for a walk in the country, I saw a little frog beginning to cross a road where there was considerable traffic. I took a stick and turned him around in the other direction towards the woods and a pond. There seemed to be an inner resistance against my attempt to save him from death. I am sure if that little frog grew up to be a writer, he would have written a book entitled "Man is Dead" . . . Some men do grow up and write books against God, entitled "God is Dead" or "God is Cruel." [393

Modern men who refuse to talk about man dying today are pleased when they talk about God dying. When they say, "God is dead," they mean that atheism is no longer the point of arrival for human reasoning. It is a point of departure for a Godless world of license. Is there a pearl to be found in this pigsty? [394

"God is Dead." Men have emancipated themselves from His sovereignty. The smell of protest drowns out the essence of worship. Many love to peer into the abyss, as Nietzsche says, and soon the abyss stares back at them. Like a bird charmed by a snake, evil enchants and conquers if for no other reason than the failure of the good to do anything. [395

Maybe they say, "God is dead" because we who believe in God theoretically are living that way practically . . . God *is* dead in any heart that does not love stricken humanity. [396

. . . Reflections On. Three reflections may be offered concerning the "God is dead" theology: First, it attracts attention. Ibsen was once quoted all over the world when he said: "Maybe two plus two equals five in the fixed stars." Chesterton answered: "How do you know there are any such things as fixed stars except by adding over and over again that two plus two equals four." The juvenile mood which writes dirty words on back fences grows up into writing books on "God is dead." Never before was there such a fuss over the mythical or the non-existent. These theologians are sure that God is dead; they know where He is buried; they have biologized in His remains—but they set a watch over His grave, as if they were momentarily expecting a Resurrection . . . Second, in the United States, the Morticians of Deity are the professors; in Europe the embalming is done by the dramatists and novelists. But under their atheism is a symbol which comes out for God. Sartre, for example, is thinking about God even when he denies Him. He who started out as a positive atheist, has now asserted: "You see, my atheism is provisional. It is due to the fact that God has not yet revealed Himself to me." Others affirm His existence under some symbol, such as un-hope in Thomas Hardy, or the emptiness and despair as with Unanuno and Valery; or the sense of guilt which survives despite all denials, as in Camus, or the law as in Kafka and the Father as in Eliot. God who is declared dead at the front door, is brought alive by the back door. The Europeans in denying God, set up a kind of humanism; a brotherhood of man without a Fatherhood of God, which would make all of us illegitimate children. The new breed of American theologians take the illogical position that we must become wholly secular, then we will find God. It is like doctors advocating a plague to discover health and economists inducing a financial crash to make everyone prosperous . . . Third, the "Death of God" is not new in history. When it does happen, it is not so much an affair of the reason as it is of the will. An adulterous husband will generally find fault with his faithful wife because she is to him a symbol of duty, morality and conscience. He thinks that if he could get rid of her, he could sin with impunity. Even Nietzsche himself who proclaimed the Death of God, manifested the same psychology; he advocated sinning and revolting to a point where the moral distinction between right and wrong would be blurred, confused and destroyed. [397

... **Resurrection.** From another point of view, God is dead . . . Every day in the Creed, we say "died and was buried." It is no news to us that God died. We believe in the Resurrection when He said, "Go, teach all nations." The answer to the atheists is not to write learned books against them but to begin to serve humanity.   [398

GOOD

... **Evil.** The good are those who try to find some good in others, and they generally do find it. The evil are those who look for the faults of others, and as a result never see their own.   [399

GOODNESS

Goodness always appears as a reproach to those who are not living right, and this reproach on the part of the sinner expresses itself in hatred and persecution. There is rarely a disrupted, frustrated soul, critical and envious of his neighbor, who is not at the same time an antireligious man.   [400

... **Hatred of.** It is not easy for normal persons to understand how goodness and truth can be hated, but they are. Truth can be hated, because it implies responsibility. Goodness is hated, because it is a reproach. If Our Blessed Lord had been tolerant and broad-minded, He would never have been crucified.   [401

... **Will.** Most people *want* to be good, but they do not *will* to be good.   [402

GOSPEL

... **Mammon.** Never before in history was the Gospel's warning about God and Mammon as clearly fulfilled as today—for the soul that has lost its God must worship Mammon. [403

GRACE

Grace is the germ of glory; it has the potencies of the beatific vision within it. [403-A

Once there is this divine romance between divinity and humanity in the person of Christ, there arises the great question confronting every human being: will he appropriate to himself this Divine Life, which is gratis and, therefore, called "grace," or will he reject it? [404

Grace is life—the life of God among men. It is that divine life which Christ as the Son of God brought to this earth. [405

... **Effect Of.** Those who have responded to the gift of grace begin to feel the presence of God in a new way. Their religion ceases to be "moralistic" in the sense which means that a man merely submits himself to a code, a law, and feels the necessity of obeying them as a duty. Religion also rises above the pietistic level on which there is a loving remembrance of Our Lord, a kind of sentimental fellow traveling, through hymns and sermons, with One who lived 1900 years ago. For although some people have found a considerable emotional fulfillment on this pietistic plane, it is not Christianity and does not become so until one enters the third stage, the Mystical. Here at last—where Christ actually dwells in our hearts, and where there is an awareness rooted in love, and where the soul feels the tremendous impact of God working on itself—here is found the joy that surpasses all understanding. [406

... Effect Of. When this actual grace of God gets into the soul, it acts something like light, shining through a Gothic window to suffuse it with a brilliance which the stained glass does not have of and by itself. [407

... Judgment. Imagine two souls appearing before the sight of God, one in the state of grace, the other in the state of sin . . . Just as a father recognizes his own son because of likeness of nature, so too Christ recognizes the soul in the state of grace in virtue of resemblance to Him, and says to the soul: "Come ye blessed of My Father: I am the natural Son, you are the adopted son. Come into the Kingdom prepared for you from all eternity." God looks into the other soul that is in the state of sin and has not that likeness, and just as a father knows his neighbor's son is not his own, so too God, looking at the sinful soul and failing to see therein the likeness of His own flesh and blood, does not recognize it as His own kind, and says to it as He said in the parable of the bridegroom "I know you not"—and it is a terrible thing not to be known by God. [408

... Life Of. A treatise on grace might be called a supernatural biology, for the laws of organic life are feeble reflections of the laws of the life of grace. The very notion of biogenesis, the law that all life must come from previous life, and can never be spontaneously generated, is a natural truth which should prepare the mind for the supernatural truth that human life can never generate divine life, but that divine life must be a gift. [409

GRATITUDE

...Children. A very interesting phenomenon in children is that gratitude or thankfulness comes relatively late in their young lives. They almost have to be taught it; if not, they are apt to grow up thinking that the world owes them a living. [410

GROWTH

One cannot put a bomb under a child and make it a man. Each thing has its own appointed law of growth, provided its roots are properly fixed. [411

GUILT

What is driving people to sleeping tablets is to some extent driving them to psychoanalytical couches—they are in flight from what is distasteful and what cannot be blotted out—and most often it is unrequited guilt. We point out these sad facts to remind those who are full of fears and anxieties that there is another remedy besides sleeping tablets, and that is consciously confronting our guilt and asking the pardon of God. Another way is to live right, so we won't have to try to forget. [412

...Forms Of. The examination of conscience, because it is concerned with guilt as an offense against love of God or neighbor, is quite distinct from attempts to cure the pathological forms of guilt which haunt some disturbed minds. The former can never be blotted out by any form of analysis or psychiatry; the latter may fail within that field and may belong to the spiritual domain, as well. Hence we must distinguish between guilt in the strict sense of the term and guilt in the broad sense of the term.   [413

...Psychiatry. Excluding what is truly morbid, irrational, and pathological, a sense of guilt does not belong solely within the competence of psychiatry. Purely psychological treatment will not cure a genuine sense of guilt. Even if the superficial sense of guilt be eliminated by autosuggestion, analysis, medicine, or persuasion, the fault that caused the guilt still remains. Psychotherapy would deceive itself if it pretended that the fault no longer existed. Hence psychiatrists must be careful not to confuse the morbid feeling of guilt, which is specific to neurotics, with an awareness of guilt which is proper to all sinners.   [414

·· H ··

HABITS

There are three kinds of dirt that can accumulate as habits
on the window of the soul to keep God's Grace from coming
in. These are carnal dirt, or inordinate love of fleshy pleasures; money dirt, or the lust of possessions; and egocentric
dirt, or selfishness and vanity. Cleaning the window of the
soul even a little brings God much closer. "Blessed are the
clean of heart for they shall see God."   [415

If we never learned habits, think of how difficult it would
be to dress. We would probably have the same trouble as a
man has taking off his trousers in an upper berth; that is one
action when a man seems to lose all resemblance to the
image and likeness of God. If there were no habits, we might
spend all day dressing. It is said that some women still do. A
child who is just learning to wash his own hands is very
clumsy with the soap; he would be that way all during life if
it were not for the ability to develop skill through habit.
                                                           [416

HANDSHAKE

A handshake is a mystery or a sacrament; there is something visible about it, namely, the clasping of hands; there is

something invisible and spiritual too, namely, the communication of friendship. [417

HAPPINESS

... Attainment Of. Happiness consists in overcoming
the bias to evil by realizing one's Divine vocation and by
overcoming the urge of nature, and this is not achieved
through the orgiastic release of primeval forces, but rather
through an *askesis* which amounts almost to violence. This is
what Our Blessed Lord had in mind when He said that the
Kingdom of Heaven suffereth violence and only the violent
will bear it away. To the Christian, the way of perfection is
the way of disipline, because he understands perfection as
the satisfaction of personality in its highest reaches—namely,
the attainment of life and truth and love, which is God.
[418

... Wealth. Want of wealth is not necessarily the cause
of unhappiness. There are more divorces, more frustrated
lives, more inner misery among the rich than among the
poor. [419

... Worldliness. How foolish to make happiness consist
in that which one day we must leave. [420

HATE

... Answer. If we go on answering hate with hate, how
will hate ever end? [421

... Communism. There exists for the first time in the
history of the world a philosophy and a political and social

system based not on love, but on hate, and that is communism. [422

...**Love.** Hate and love spring from the same passion, as laughter and sorrow drink from the same fountain of tears.
[423

HEAVEN

It is very likely that there will be many surprises in heaven. Many people will be there that we never expected to find, and many will not be there whom we expected to see; and finally, we probably will be most surprised to find ourselves there. [424

HELL

Hell is not related to an evil life, as is generally supposed, as a spanking is related to an act of disobedience, for a spanking need not necessarily follow disobedience, and rarely does in juvenile circles. Rather, hell is related to an evil life as blindness is related to the plucking out of an eye. [425

Hell is the ego, sated with its own satisfied wishes, having to consume itself forever with no hope of release. [426

...**Denial Of.** If a man has led a very wicked life, he does not want to be disturbed in his wrongdoings by harsh words about justice. His wish that there be no final punishment for his crimes thus becomes father to the thought that there is no such thing as hell. That is why the wicked man denies hell, whereas the saint never denies it, but only fears it. [427

...Earth. Some say we have our hell on this earth. We do. We can start it here, but it does not finish here.   [428

...Love. Hell is a place where there is no love, for God is love . . . The souls in hell hate themselves most for wounding Perfect Love . . . It is not that God would not forgive them. It is rather they will not forgive themselves . . . The evil person incessantly wants a recasting of values.   [429

...Reality Of. The church has never altered one single iota the belief in an eternal hell as taught by her founder, Our Lord and Savior, Jesus Christ. In adherence to His divine testimony, the Church teaches first that hell is a demand of justice, and second, that hell is a demand of love. First of all, once it is recognized that the moral order is grounded on justice, then retribution beyond the grave becomes a necessity . . . The teaching of Our Blessed Lord bears out this demand of justice, for His doctrine was not merely an amiable gospel of indifference as His own life was not one of sentimental good-naturedness. He very distinctly taught that men might do things which would prove their undoing . . . The very fact that He poured out His life's blood to redeem us from sin could only mean that sin might have such a terrible consequence as hell.   [430

...Reason. Why do souls go to hell? In the last analysis, they go to hell for only one reason: because they refuse to love. Souls do not go to hell just because they break the commandments, for why should the breaking of a commandment merit hell? God does not forbid lying, murder, dishonesty, adultery, to amuse Himself. They are not arbitrary commands. He forbids them because they hurt us. Their violation is a sign of our anti-love. [431

HOLINESS

... **Saints.** Saints never speak of their holiness; that is why it is very difficult to portray a truly religious man on the stage. [432

HOME

... **Children.** The home is the schoolhouse for affection wherein a mother completes the work that was begun when the child was born. [433

... **Respect.** Let there be in the home a respect for the partner, not on the basis of whether the partner gives pleasure, but because the partner is a person, and a gift of God to be loved as one's own flesh. Then there will be less cowardice and surrender, more courage and more faith and a better America. But to love another for God's sake, we must really believe in God. [434

HOMES

... **Broken.** Thirteen million youths in the United States are half-orphans. Some see drunken fathers, others see neurotic mothers. The want of fidelity and love in the home makes them as much despair of loyalty in private matters as honesty in public. [435

HONOR

Making honor the goal of life is to make our happiness dependent upon others, and happiness should be something no one can take away. Furthermore, if honor is the ideal of life, then disgrace is the only sin. [436

... **Man.** Human beings are like sponges. Each human being can stand so much honor, as a sponge can hold so much water. Both quickly reach a point of saturation. When the sponge passes that point, it drips; when a man passes that point, the honor wears the man. [437

... **Reputation.** It is really not honor based on virtue which men seek today, but rather reputation, which is measured more by its width than its depth. [438

HOSPITALITY

There is a legend to the effect that one day a traveler came to the tent of Abraham. Abraham gave him his bed, served him his best lamb, his choicest wines, but the visitor did nothing but grumble, complain, and groan. Finally, after three days, Abraham could not stand it any longer, and he chased away the visitor. God spoke to Abraham, saying, "Abraham, I put up with that man for fifty years. Cannot you put up with him for three days?" [439

HUMANISM

As humanism leaves unexplained the intelligibility of the universe, so does it also leave unexplained the aspiration to perfect happiness which exists in the human will. Men generally recognize that neither in their own reason, nor in their own will, nor in the times in which they live, is the secret of happiness. That is why the Greek and Roman mythology put the Golden Age in the remote past, as Virgil did in his *Fourth Eclogue,* or else in the remote future as do the Utopians and evolutionists of the present day, or the Communists, who expectantly look to an order when the dialectic will no longer apply and therefore where the transcendence of communism will be impossible.   [440

HUMANITY

... **Two Groups.** Humanity is divided into two groups, namely, the old humanity which is still governed by the flesh, and the new, regenerated humanity which is governed by the Spirit: the humanity of goodness, love of God, love of neighbor. The area of indifference is narrowing. The world is rapidly dividing into opposite poles of good and evil. The good are beginning to be better, and the evil are becoming worse.   [441

HUMAN RIGHTS

Too long have we in the council of nations been trying to preserve the fruits of Christianity without preserving its roots. The task is hopeless. In vain will we seek to preserve the liberties and rights of human beings throughout the world unless we keep in hearts and minds and consciences, the God from whom all powers come.   [442

HUMILITY

The modern man is humble, not with the old humility which made a man doubt his power, but with the new humility that makes a man doubt his humanity.   [443

Humility is not a want of moral force; rather humility is a recognition of the truth about ourselves. To explore the

Truth in all its complexity there must come moments when we confess ignorance, when we frankly admit that we were mistaken or bigoted, or prejudiced. [444

Being humble implies that our eye recognizes the need of light, our reason admits the need of faith, and our whole being the guidance of the Eternal Law of God. [445

Humility does not consist so much in humbling ourselves before others as it does in recognizing our own littleness in comparison to what we ought to be. [446

... Discovery. No man discovers anything big unless he makes himself small. [447

... Egotism. The humble violet that grows close to the earth is more praised by poets than the sunflower that always turns its head to the spotlight. [448

... Goodness. No man is good unless he is humble; and humility is a recognition of truth concerning oneself. A man who thinks he is greater than he actually is is not humble, but a vain and boastful fool. How can any man claim prerogatives over conscience, and over history, and over society and the world, and still claim he is "meek and humble of heart"? But if He is God as well as man, His language falls into place and everything that He says is intelligible. [449

... Heaven. Heaven is very high, but the gate to it is very low. To enter we must stoop; bending the ego is the condition of entering therein, and that requires the virtue of humility. [450

... Meaning Of. Humility does not mean letting other people walk over you. Humility is not passivity, submissiveness, nor underestimation of oneself; it is not condemnation, nor a belittling of oneself; it is not an enemy of greatness striving for the stars, for when God became man He gave the Counsel: 'Be ye perfect as your Heavenly Father is perfect.' Humility is not a self-awareness that one is humble, for then it becomes pride; humility is not a self-contempt that prepares for gloom, or cynicism, nor is it believing that our talents are less valuable than they really are. A man six foot three who is praised for being so tall is not humble when he says: 'Oh no, I am really only four feet four.' Humility is truth about ourselves; it is a virtue by which one does not esteem himself to be more than he really is.   [451

... Praise. The humble man . . . receives praise as the window receives light, not as the battery receives a current.
[452

... Socrates. Few have the humility of Socrates, who was lampooned in the play *The Clouds* by Aristophanes. Socrates went to the theater and stood up during the entire spectacle, so that everyone could see how true the caricature really was.   [453

HUMOR
... Saints. Saints have a sense of humor. I do not mean only canonized saints, but rather that great army of staunch and solid Christians to whom everything and every incident speaks a story of God's love. A saint can be defined as one who has a divine sense of humor, for a saint never takes this world seriously as the lasting city.   [454

HUNGER

...East; West. The whole world is dying of hunger. The Eastern world is dying of hunger of body; the Western world is dying of hunger of soul ... the Western world will be saved by feeding the East. [455

·· **I** ··

IDEALS

Ideals were always held up to men and still are, but an ideal without personification is without appeal. No one can fall in love with a theorem of geometry.　　　　　[456

　... **Duty.** Shorn of an ideal, the mere doing of duty can become a high form of self-centered egotism.　　　[457

IDEAS

　... **Strength.** The mind is strengthened by a strong idea. An English professor of psychiatry tested weight lifters . . . He hypnotized them and told them they were strong. They lifted 142 pounds . . . He hypnotized them again and told them that they were weak. They lifted only 29 pounds. The idea of weakness induced weakness in action. The mind was exhausted before the body. At the time of the San Francisco earthquake, 30 people who had been in bed for 30 years got up and walked . . . Get wrong ideas in your head and they come out as bad actions. It is nonsense to say that it does not make any difference what you think or believe, it all depends on how you act. If you think about robbing a bank, you will end up robbing one. Keep the mind clean and the body will keep clean.　　　　　[458

...**Truths.** Feelings, emotions, and mystical states are individual; ideas and truths are universal. The intellect will once more return to philosophy when the true critical spirit returns—that is, when philosophers see that the anti-intellectualism of the present day is a protest against a distorted view of the intellect which was held by the mechanists, but not by the traditional intellectualists of the ages.   [459

IMAGINATION

...**Children.** The child is a voyager without any baggage. He lives in the present and imagines it to be eternal. He can mount a broomstick and imagine himself to be King of infinite space.   [460

IMMACULATE CONCEPTION

...**Virgin Birth.** The Immaculate Conception and the Virgin Birth were to the beginning of a new humanity something like what a lock is to a canal, the former in a special way. If a ship is sailing on a polluted canal and wishes to transfer itself to clear waters on a higher level, it must pass through a device which locks out the polluted waters and raises the ship to the higher position. Then the other gate of the lock is lifted, and the ship rides on the new, clear waters, taking none of the polluted waters with it. Mary's Immaculate Conception was like that lock, inasmuch as, through her, humanity passed from the lower level of the sons of Adam to the higher level of the sons of God.   [461

IMMORTALITY

On this earth we have merely a note; the melody is beyond.   [462

That very life of God that passes from Father to Son in the eternal generation of the Trinity, now passes into the world and assumes a human nature like our own, graces it with the plenitude of His divinity, and gives us that message of hope: "I am come that you may have life and that in abundance"—not the physical life which dies, but the spiritual life which endureth unto life everlasting.   [463

... **Consequences of Denial.** The denial of immortality gives death a double mastery, first over the person who denies survival, though he needs must die, and second by leading him to repudiate family life, which is now regarded as a mere hindrance to the pleasures of the brief hour of life. It is a historical fact that in times of disaster, epidemic, bombings, etc., some individuals who have no eternal values to sustain them, seeing the lease on life about to run out, plunge into orgies of debauchery.   [464

... **Mortality.** Our mortality is frightening to us largely because we can contemplate *immortality*, and we have a dim suspicion that we have lost the immortality that once belonged to us. We ought to have it; yet we have it not. Something has interfered. We are not all we ought to be. If death were merely a physical *must*, we would not fear it; our fear comes from the moral fact that we know we *ought* not to die.   [465

... **New Birth.** If we are to live in a higher life, we must die to the lower life; if we live in the lower life of this world, we die to a higher life which is Christ. To put the whole law in the beautiful paradox of Our Divine Lord: If we wish to save our life, we must lose it, that is, if we wish to save it for eternity, we must lose it for time; if we wish to save it for the Father's mansions, we must lose it for this dull world; if we wish to save it for perfect happiness, we must lose it for fleeting pleasure of mortality. [466

IMPATIENCE

A person who believes in nothing beyond this world is very impatient, because he has only a limited time in which to satisfy his sordid wants. [467

INCARNATION

What men call the Incarnation is but the union of two natures, the divine and the human, in a single person who governs both. This is not difficult to understand; for what is man but a sample, at an immeasurably lower level, of a union of two totally different substances, one material and the other immaterial, one the body, the other the soul, under the regency of a single human personality? [468

INDEPENDENCE

... False. All quarrels, disagreements, wars, strifes, and dissensions begin with a false declaration of independence—independence from God and independence from fellowman. [469

INDIFFERENCE

... Decision. Man can either mount upward to the peak of eternity or else slip backward to the chasms of despair and frustration. Yet there are many who think there is yet another alternative, namely, that of indifference. They think

that, just as bears hibernate for a season in a state of sus-
pended animation, so they, too, can sleep through life without choosing to live for God or against Him. But hibernation
is no escape; winter ends, and one is then forced to make a
decision—indeed, the very choice of indifference itself is a
decision.   [470

... Socialism.   As men become indifferent to right and
wrong, disorder and chaos increase, and the State steps in to
organize the chaos by force. Dictatorships arise in such a
fashion. Such is the essence of Socialism, the compulsory
organization of chaos.   [471

... Tolerance.   Indifferent are those who deny that there
is any such thing as good or evil, or who have no philosophy
of life and who accept no goal or purpose. Right and wrong
to them are merely points of view. "Tolerance" is identified
with an equal value to right and wrong, truth and error,
virtue and vice. The indifferent generally boast that they are
"open-minded"; they are willing to hear all sides, but refuse
to accept any. Their minds are so "open" that ideas pass right
through.   [472

INDIGNATION

Never once is Our Blessed Lord indignant against those
who are already, in the eyes of society, below the level of law
and respectability. He attacked only the sham indignation of
those who dwelt more on the sin than the sinner and who
felt pleasantly virtuous, because they had found someone
more vicious than they.   [473

INDIVIDUALISM

When 10,000 run headlong toward an abyss, he who runs
from it seems to the others to be in flight.   [474

Karl Marx understood better than even some in America the inherent source of right. Marx did not like democracy because he said that democracy is founded on a principle that every man has a soul, independently of any society or class. Marx said, "I contend that only the class has rights. *An individual has no value whatever unless he is a member of the revolutionary class."*   [475

... **Environment.** In previous ages, there were individuals who were weak mentally or even evil, but society was strong and it sustained the weak. The individual was less apt to crack because the environment was more stable; today, the environment is polluted, and the individual has not that social cushion to save him in his psychosis and neurosis.   [476

... **Persons.** The difference between an individual and a person is this: individuals are replaceable, and persons are not . . . you go to buy oranges in a store and say, "No, this one is bad. Give me another." But you cannot say that about children. A child is a person—unique, incommunicable, irreplaceable—that is why there is so much sorrow in a mother when one is lost. It is a person and an immortal soul that has departed.   [477

... **Worth.** In lower nature such as the animal kingdom, it is only the species that are important, for nature seems to be heedless of the number of individuals that perish. But in humanity, it is the individual who has worth.   [478

INFALLIBILITY

The enemies of the Papacy fail to make a distinction between infallibility and impeccability. Infallibility means

freedom from error, impeccability means freedom from
sin.   [479

INFIDELITY

Husbands who are unfaithful will beat their wives who
are faithful. Wives who are unfaithful will accuse their
husbands of infidelity.   [480

INFINITE

...**Man's Yearning.** The squirrel is as happy as he can
be in a tree with nuts, and a cow is contented in the field.
But our hearts, which were made for the Infinite, yearn for
"more and more"; perhaps that is one of the reasons why
evolution has so much appealed to us, because it assures in
an indefinite future a perfection which we do not have at the
present time.   [481

INFINITY

...**Man.** God made this world too small for us! . . .
Each moment we bump into the walls of the universe and
skin our shins on its fences. This is the basic cause of all
yearning and all suffering. We were made for the infinite.
We have wings on our soul but we beat them against the
cage of our body and the triviality of our cities.   [482

INSTINCT

...**Salvation.** Would a duck have the instinct to swim if
there were no water? Would a baby cry for nourishment if
there were no such thing as food? . . . And would there be
in you a craving for unending life, perfect truth and ecstatic
love unless Perfect Life and Truth and Love existed?   [483

INTELLECT

The light of man's intelligence is like the twilight compared to that of God and angels, and hence his intellectual vision is obscure.   [484

... **Religion.** The way we live has an influence on the way we think. This is not a denial of the intellectual factors in belief, but merely an attempt to emphasize a neglected element. Some people imagine that they can bring a person to divine love merely by answering a doubt he has expressed. They assume that men are irreligious only because they are ignorant; that if atheists read a few good books or listened to a few choice arguments in favor of divinity, they would immediately embrace the faith. Religion seems to them to be a thing to be *known*, rather than a personality to be *embraced* and lived and loved . . . Intellectual knowledge is not the "one thing necessary": not all the Ph.D.'s are saints, and the ignorant are not demons. Indeed, a certain type of education may simply turn a man from a stupid egotist into a clever egotist, and of the two the former has the better chance of salvation.   [485

... **Truth.** What a man will intellectually accept depends to a great extent on what a man *is* or what he wants to be. The will, instead of admitting a truth presented to the mind, can ward it off and bar it out. God's pursuit of a mind is bound to fail unless the mind is also in pursuit of goodness.   [486

INTELLIGENCE

... **Facts.** The mark of intelligence is the ability to correlate facts, to see the relation between them, to be able to judge their value, to have standards of comparison. An encyclopedia has a vast store of facts, but an encyclopedia is not educated. Aristotle contended that those who had a good memory generally had a poor judgment. This was his own way of distinguishing between memory and true knowledge.

[487

INTELLIGIBILITY

Intelligibility is hidden in the universe, otherwise the human mind, which at the beginning is a blank, would never attain to the intelligible.   [488

INTROSPECTION

Most of us do not like to look inside ourselves for the same reason we do not like to open a letter that has bad news.

[489

. . . **Fear.**   Some people are afraid ever to look into their consciences, for fear of what they might find. But introspection is to the soul what diagnosis is to the body—the first necessary step toward health. The Prodigal Son "entered into himself" before he was able to resolve to admit his mistakes to his father.   [490

INVOLVEMENT

Once a man ceases to be of service to his neighbor, he begins to be a burden to him; it is only a step from refusing to live with others to refusing to live for others.   [491

. . . **Compassion.**   In the parable of the Good Samaritan it is said that a priest and a Levite passed by the wounded

man and help was given him by one of another race—
namely, the Samaritan. We do not know whatever happened
to the priest and the Levite, but it is very likely that they
went into Jerusalem and reported the condition of the dying
man to a social service agency. [492

· · J · ·

JEALOUSY

Jealousy is the tribute which mediocrity pays to genius.

[493

JESUS

The Savior turns out the buyers and sellers from the
Temple and then takes a child upon His knees and says that
he will enter the Kingdom of Heaven before the wise university professors. He washes the feet of disciples who seek
first place at table, talks freely to women whom the whole
nation hates, and intervenes to protect an adulteress from
stoning at the hands of those whose adultery has not yet
been found out. The announcement of His Incarnation was
made to a Virgin; but the announcement of His Resurrection from the dead was made to a converted sinner.   [494

... Purpose. The purpose of His life, He said, was to
pay a ransom for the liberation of the slaves of sin; this was a
divine "must" that was laid upon Him when He came into
the world. His death was offered in payment for evil. If men
were only in error, He might have been a teacher fenced in
by all the comforts of life; and after having taught the theory

of pain, He would die on a soft bed. But then He would have left no other message than a code to obey. But if men were in sin, He would be a redeemer and His message would be "follow Me," to share in the fruit of that redemption.

[495

... **Savior.** No teacher who ever lived told those who heard him that the rejection of his words would mean their damnation. Even those who believe that Christ was only a teacher would scruple at this judgment about receiving His message. But being primarily a savior, the alternative was understandable. To reject the savior was to reject salvation.

[496

... **Savior.** This Child came not to save people from insecurity, or to make them rich and powerful, but to save them from their sins. Hence He was given the name of Jesus, which means Savior.

[497

JESUS CHRIST
... **His Divinity.** If we are to find the secret of His Timelessness, the simplicity of His Wisdom, the transforming power of His Doctrine, we must go out beyond time to the Timelessness, beyond the complex to the Perfect, beyond change to the Changeless, out beyond the world to the Perfect God.

[498

JOURNALISM
... **Responsibility.** If a moral man sat down to decide for himself the one secular profession he would approach with the greatest reluctance, because of the responsibility it

involved, that profession would be the publishing of a news-paper.   [499

JOY

... Pleasure. Pleasure comes from without, but joy comes from within, and it is, therefore, within the reach of everyone in the world.   [500

... Pleasure; Happiness. Joy is not the same as pleasure or happiness. A wicked and evil man may have pleasure, while any ordinary mortal is capable of being happy. Pleasure generally comes from things, and always through the senses; happiness comes from humans through fellowship . . . Pleasure is quick and violent, like a flash of lightning. Joy is steady and abiding, like a fixed star. Pleasure depends on external circumstances, such as money, food and travel. Joy is independent of them.   [501

... Source. To pass from sadness to joy requires a birth, a moment of travail and labor, for no one ever mounts to a higher level of life without death to the lower. Before such an ascent, conscience, for a moment, has a hard, stern work to do. Pearls come from the bottom of the water, gold from the depths of the earth, and the great joys of life are to be found in the recesses of a contrite, broken heart.   [502

JUDGMENT

The separation of people into sheep and goats will take place only at the Last Day. Until then we are forbidden to make the classification.   [503

Nothing so much encourages a merciful judgment of others as the Divine warning that as we judge others, so shall we be judged. [504

...**Human.** Why should we go on saying: "I am the only judge; I am the only standard of truth." These statements remind one of the tourist who, passing through one of the galleries of Florence, remarked to the guide: "I don't think much of these pictures." To which the guide answered: "These pictures are not here for your judgment; they are your judges." So, too, your rejection of the truths beyond reason are the judge of your humility, your love of truth, and your knowledge. [505

...**Love.** Why is there more joy in Heaven for the repentant sinner than for the righteous? Because God's attitude is not judgment but *love*. [506

...**Man.** In order to judge others we must be inside them and outside them, but only God can do this. Our neighbors are just as impenetrable to us as we are to them. Judgment on our part, then, would be wrong, for to judge without a mandate is unjust. Our Lord alone has a mandate to judge; we have not. [507

JUSTICE

The breast of every man bears a silent court of justice. [508

JUVENILE DELINQUENCY

... Parents who recognize no authority above them have children who do not recognize their authority. In a machine, when the big gears fail to function, the little gears go out of order . . . The farmer who does not obey nature's laws as regards the seasons should not wonder why he has bad crops.

[509

. . . **Delinquent Parents.** The principle cause of delinquent children is delinquent parents. Almighty God has given children to the parents as so much clay to be molded according to the Divine Image. When a child is born, a crown is made for it in Heaven; woe to those parents if that crown is eternally unused.

[510

. . . **Reasons For.** In a very few instances do juvenile delinquents steal food or clothing; they steal because they want to satisfy their pampered egos. Having never learned the relationship existing between effort and reward, the youth now substitutes spoils for rewards. The basic right to *pursue* happiness now becomes for him the right to *have* happiness at the cost of others.

[511

··K··

KENNEDY, JOHN F.

I was in Rome in the first shattering shock of the death of President Kennedy. The suddenness of his death came like an earthquake; it affected so many and in such magnitude that one could not find a heart to console—others, too, were inconsolable. In lesser bereavements, there are those who are not involved, but then there were no others to wipe away tears, for they too were mourners. [512

...His Death. We have walked with pleasure for many a mile and we have smiled and smiled and learned nothing. But what a vista of the mystery which lies in the heart of the world's redemption was unveiled when we, as a people, walked with sorrow! [513

...Tribute. It took a Lincoln's blood to write a nation; it has taken a Kennedy's blood to prepare for the equality of men in that same nation . . . On a brighter Easter day, we shall see that our national brotherhood was purchased by the blood of a victim—John Fitzgerald Kennedy. In the future, too, at the other end of a pool where the image of the victim Lincoln is reflected, there will be cast another monument, the heroic image of the victim Kennedy, for both were great, not by what was done *by* them, but what was done *through* them . . . Above our national figures, these two Presidents of Sorrow stand forever near the Man of Sorrows saying: "I will stand here at Thy side; despise my nation not."   [514

KNOWLEDGE

. . . **Immorality.** It is very interesting to examine the effects of immorality on knowledge . . . by studying the different insights, judgments, and conclusions of writers before and after they have repudiated the moral law. It is extremely interesting to read the writings of reputedly learned men before and after they have divorced their wives and married again. It hardly seems as if the same minds were at work.   [515

. . . **Genius; Reading.** It has been said that some of the great geniuses of the past never read half as much as the mediocre geniuses today, but what they read they understood and incorporated into a much deeper dimension of knowledge.   [516

. . . **Light.** Knowledge is as necessary as light. In fact it is like light: it is in itself devoid of color, taste and odor and it should be kept pure and without admixture. If it comes to us through the medium of prejudice, hate, or uncontrolled passions, it is discolored and adulterated.   [517

. . . **Unity.** Because you learn the soliloquy of Hamlet by heart does not preclude me or anyone else from learning it. In fact, the more of us who know the poem, the more we are united with one another.   [518

· · L · ·

LANGUAGE

...**Communication.** Words should be like windows:
We should be able to see through them. They should not be
like curtains which veil the inside of the mind from the
outside of the lips. An equal sign should always be made
between what is in the mind and what is on the lips; if we
cannot make the equation, the words should not be said.

[519

LAUGHTER

The wonderful madness called laughter is found only in
man. Nothing in lower creation produces anything resem-
bling a laugh. Valleys do not smile, and horses do not laugh,
for it is a positive break with everything below him in
creation; it is a break with matter, it is the beginning of the
spirit. Man is the only joker in the deck of Nature.   [520

LAW

...**Tradition.** You cannot think without going back to
the storehouse of your memory, so, too, civilization has a
memory, and our country has a memory and a tradition.
That tradition is freedom within the law and not outside of
it.   [521

LAZINESS

...Mental. Laziness manifests itself, for example, in limiting reading to pictures. It used to be that a picture illustrated a text; now a text is used to illustrate or explain a picture. [522

...Spiritual. The Old and the New Testament differ on the subject of spiritual laziness. In the Old Testament, a man was condemned because he did wrong; in the New Testament, a man is condemned who leaves a good undone. [523

LEARNING

...Capacity. As the stomach can suffer from indigestion, so can the mind. If too many ideas are poured into it and there are not sufficient juices of the intellect to absorb them, a queer kind of literary constipation follows. [524

...Desire For. Those who had a taste for philosophy in the days of Aristotle, a yearning for poetry in the days of Dante, for metaphysics in the days of Abelard, and for sacred science when the monasteries held all the treasures of knowledge, spared no effort to absorb learning. But now that reading is accessible in every drugstore and city corner, the discrimination has decreased with the availability. [525

LEISURE

The modern man has more leisure than the men of a century ago, but he knows less what to do with it. [526

LENT

... Penance. Lent is the penitential season, a time when men once put on hair shirts, sacrificing any hope of bodily ease for 40 days. G. K. Chesterton once said that St. Thomas A. Becket wore a hair shirt under his purple, so that people might have the benefit of his purple and he might have the benefit of penance. [527

LIBERTY

... Liberals. A river must be happier than a swamp because it has banks and boundaries; a swamp is a valley of liberty that lost its shores and became "liberal." [528

... Responsibility. Liberty is no heirloom. It requires the daily bread of self denial, the salt of law and, above all, the backbone of acknowledging responsibility for our deeds. [529

LICENSE

The logic of license is frightening. If all things are allowable, then man becomes a slave to his own freedom. [530

... Carnal. An age of carnal license is always an age of political anarchy. The foundations of social life are shaken at the very moment when the foundations of family life are destroyed. [531

LIFE

Life is a tremendous drama in which one may say, "Aye" or "Nay" to his eternal destiny. To admit light to the eye,

music to the ear and food to the stomach is to perfect each of
these organs; so too, to admit Truth to the mind and Power
to the will is to make us more than a creature, namely, a
partaker of the Divine Nature.   [532

Life is a vertical dimension expressed in the soaring spire,
or in the leaping fountain, both of which suggest that earth,
history, and nature must be left behind to seek union with
the Eternal.   [533

... **Compartments Of.** Man's life nowadays is divided
into many compartments which remain ununited and unin-
tegrated. A businessman's business has no connection with
his life in the family—so little in fact that his wife (his
"little wife") is kept ignorant of her husband's income. As
there is no connection between a man's profession and the
rest of his daily existence, neither is there a connection
between his daily life and his religion. This chopping up of
life into watertight compartments becomes more disastrous
as occupation and work are related, less and less, to a strictly
human ideal; mechanization plays a catastrophic role.   [534

... **Future.** The man who does not believe in a future
life has to take this one very seriously.   [535

... **Higher.** Is there not something higher that can come
down to man, on the one condition that man die to himself?
The rose has no right to say there is no higher life than itself.
Man has no right to say there is no higher life than himself.
Two little tadpoles were playing in the water. One little
tadpole said to the other, "I think I will stick my head above

the water and see if there is anything else in this world."
The first tadpole said, "Don't be silly. You mean to say there
is something else in this world besides water?" Many human
beings are like tadpoles in the sense that they deny there is
anything above them into which they can be incorporated.

[536

...**Meaning.** There is nothing that so much under-
mines the minds of people as the loss of the meaning of life.
After all, if we do not know why we are here, why go on
living?   [537

...**Meaninglessness.** It is the meaninglessness of life
that makes it wearisome.   [538

...**Pleasure.** Some would say life is a snare and an
illusion, promising what it cannot deliver. They then im-
merse themselves in adding one finite pleasure to another,
mostly carnal, in the hope of reaching the infinite. But they
are doomed to failure, for all they are doing is adding zeros.
In vain will any man think he will produce the best melody
by picking up a succession of violins.   [539

...**Purpose.** Life may be like a game of cards; we cannot
help the hand that is dealt us, but we can help the way we
play it.   [540

...**Purpose.** No one can have two final purposes in life
any more than he can walk to the right and left at the same
time.   [541

... Purpose.   People live 10, 20, 30, 50 years without a plan. No wonder they find their existence humdrum and tiresome. If they were farmers, they would probably plant wheat one week, root it up and plant barley next; then dig up the barley and plant watermelon; then dig up the watermelon another week and plant oats—and when fall comes around, they would have no harvest. If they repeated that process for years, they could go crazy.   [542

... Reason for Living.   There is not much purpose in living until one has decided why one is alive at all. When a normal person sees a gadget, he asks: "What is it for?" He asks the same question of himself. As a house is built to be lived in, a church made for worship, medicine made to restore health, and schools to communicate knowledge, so, too, man is made for something. Nothing that satisfies a part of us can be our final end; hence food, honor, sex could not be the principal or final end of man, because these satisfy only a part of him. Furthermore, these things are very often nothing but means to an end.   [543

... Record.   Life is like a cash register, in that every account, every thought, every deed, like every sale, is registered and recorded.   [544

LIGHT

Science today has found out that the atom is not just a solid piece of matter; rather, it is mostly space in which there is electricity or light. Matter is light. There are two kinds of light in the world; one is bottled light; the other is unbottled light. Bottled light is matter, such as hinges, doors, and sealing wax. Unbottled light is illumination, such as we find in a candle or a bulb. The whole universe is light, either potential or actual. That is why Sir James Jeans in his work, *The Universe Around Us,* said that the most scientific and accurate description that has ever been given of creation is that found in Genesis: God said, "Let there be light, and light was made." [545

LIKING

... Loving. You may not *like* somebody, but you can still *love,* because loving is a duty; it is good for your soul, and it also glorifies God. If you do an injury to someone you do not *like,* you will dislike him still more; if you do a favor to someone you do not like, you will love him more. [546

LIMITATIONS

As soon as we begin to see our own limitations, we perceive perfection in others. [547

LINCOLN

George Washington will always be the father of our country; but Lincoln must always be considered its savior. [548

LISTENING

One can be impolite to God by absorbing all the conversation, and by changing the words of Scripture from "speak, Lord, Thy servant hears" to "Listen, Lord, Thy servant speaks." [549

LONELINESS

Loneliness is overcome by praying for others.   [550

... Confession. The most unfortunate mortals are those who shed their tears in silence and find no one to wipe those tears away. How many men and women there are in the world who, through sin, have felt themselves alone, cast off from everyone, who in their inmost heart have felt the need of some sanctuary into which they might retire for consolation and direction. Our cities are full of souls who are constantly crying out, "What can I do?" and to these and the millions who are craving for someone who will understand and pardon, as Christ understood and pardoned weak Peter and sensuous Magdalene, the confessional is the answer.   [551

LOVE

Love that is happier if it meets only one who needs help than if it met ten, and happiest if it met none at all, is not love.   [552

... Anxiety. Anxiety is present in all love. And every human being must love or go crazy, because no man is sufficient for himself.   [553

... Being Loved. The Word is the Perfection of the Father. The Father, therefore, loves the Word, His Son. All love has two terms; he who loves and he who is loved. I love and I am loved. Between us there is something; it is not my love, it is not His love; it is *our* love . . . It is best expressed as a breath of love, which does not pass away as our love, but which subsists; and this subsisting love is the Holy

142

Spirit . . . One in Nature, three in Persons, really distinct, one from the other in virtue of the relations which separate them, yet all consubstantial in the one nature; such is the Blessed Trinity. [554

. . . **Body; Soul.** Love is psychosomatic; that is, it involves both body and soul. Love in man and what is called love in an animal are not the same. The animal lives by mechanical instincts and biological urges alone, but man freely chooses his loves. [555

. . . **Carnal.** When carnal love breaks down, then Christian love must step into the breach. The other person is then regarded not as the condition of one's *happiness* but as the condition of one's *salvation.* [556

. . . **Christ.** Because we start with the person of Christ in His Mystical Body, we believe not through fear, but with love. One cannot love dialectical materialism or ethical cosmopolitanism, nor pragmatic humanism, but one can love a person. Between our created personality and His uncreated personality there is a bond of love. So inseparable are the two that Our Lord did not communicate to Peter the power of ruling and governing His Church until three times Peter had told Our Lord that he loved Him above all else. [557

. . . **Death.** In vain does one attempt to make the intensity of an emotion a compensation for the meaninglessness of life . . . The couple begins to feel lonely together as they cling desperately to the one thing in which they find distraction, the body without the soul . . . In such love where each moves in his own orbit, bound to the other either by habit or by the common burden of discontent, anyone can understand why Freud identified *Eros* and *Thanatos*, love and death, for such love, having denied the soul and God, has no other destiny than death. As Andre Malraux said of D. H. Lawrence's Lady Chatterley, "She clings to sex in the face of disgust and death." For such reason did Baudelaire describe such love as "sitting on a skull."   [558

...**Depth Of.**   We are like rivers; the more ground we cover, the less deep is the water of our affection. Hence we must save our love for those who are *beneath* us, rather than for those who are above. Those who are above us can do without our love; they already have others to give it to them.   [559

...**Divine.**   Human love can be understood, explained, run down to its source like a mountain stream which can be traced to a spring in the rocks. But Divine Love is infinite. If we start with the stream—in Holy Communion or in prayer —we soon discover that it runs into the ocean of inexhausti- ble delights. What we know about love is a minute drop in that ocean. God's love existed before the world began; it will exist after we go; our hearts can hold only its merest particles, as in such loves as Romeo's for Juliet or Dante's for his Beatrice. Love eludes our greatest poets' words, and even the mystics' writings do not capture it.   [560

...**Enemies.**   What you love about yourself is the image of God in you; what you do not love about yourself is the ruination of that image. We are to love our neighbor that way. We are to love the sinner, but hate the sin. We must always love him as a sinner. We love the Communists, but hate Communism; we love our enemies, but hate their enmity of Justice and Truth. The erring person we receive into the treasury of our souls, but never the error into the treasury of our wisdom.   [561

. . . Environment Of. As a homeless waif is denied many blessings such as food, clothing and shelter because he is outside of the environment of love, so your life will be without great happiness, if it is outside of that Great Love that came to this earth and said, 'Love one another as I have loved you.'   [562

. . . Experience. What some people love is not a person, but the experience of being in love. The first is irreplaceable; the second is not. As soon as the glands cease to act with their pristine force, couples who identified emotionalism and love claim they no longer love one another. If such is the case they never loved the other person in the first place; they only loved being loved, which is the highest form of egotism.   [563

. . . Heart. The tragedy of the world is that so many are unloved. Roses always look beautiful and smell sweet, and hence they are a prize to be possessed. Sweetbriar, however, has fragrant leaves, and they are never so fragrant as when it rains. The common people of the world are like these leaves; they have something fragrant about them, particularly when the days are dark and clouded and rain falls in their lives. Anyone can love a rose; but it takes a great heart to love a leaf.   [564

... Humanity. Our Lord never said, "Love humanity." It is too vague and allows the individual to escape. Lovers of "humanity" or "the people" often vicariously enjoy the fruits of an idealistic worship, which in the individual instance they make a mockery. It is not unknown that lovers of the brotherhood of man without the Fatherhood of God pay their maids seventeen dollars a week. [565

... Imperfections. When we find imperfections in people we generally stop loving them. This may be the very reason they remain imperfect, because they have no one to love them into perfection. [566

... Judgment. There are three different ways in which we may judge others; with our passions, our reason and our faith. Our passions induce us to love those who love us; our reason makes us love all people within certain limits; our faith makes us love everyone, including those who do us harm and who are our enemies. [567

... Loving. It is not of great moment to be constantly asking ourselves if we love our neighbor. What is important is to act out that love. We learn to walk by walking, to play by playing and to love by loving. If we do anybody whom we hate a good turn, we find that we hate him less; if we do him an evil turn, we discover that we hate him more. Doing kind acts to people makes us find all people lovable. And if love is not there, we put it there and then everyone becomes lovable. [568

... Men; Women. A difference between the love of a man and the love of a woman is that a man will always give

146

reasons for loving, but a woman gives no reasons for loving. A man will say, "I love you because you are beautiful; I love you because your teeth are pearly; I love you because you make good shortening bread; I love you because you are sweet." The woman just says, "I love you." [569

... **Mothers.** A mother must love each offspring as if it were the only one in all the world. [570

... **Nature Of.** It is the nature of all love to desire to become one with that which is loved. God loves man. God became man and appeared in the habit and form of man, as Jesus Christ. There is something about all human affection which wants the "I" to be absorbed in another. True love is born of both a need and an emptiness which urge the hunger to be satisfied at the storehouse of another. This need is a proof of our creatureliness and of our basic need for God. [571

... **Of Country.** Love of country needs once more to be revived, otherwise we shall perish for no other crime than because we refused to love. [572

... **Of Enemies.** If a box is filled with salt it cannot be filled with sand, and if our hearts are filled with hatred of our neighbor, how can God fill them with His love? It is just as simple as that. There can be and there will be no mercy toward us unless we ourselves are merciful. The real test of the Christian then is not how much he loves his friends, but how much he loves his enemies. [573

... Of God. When you find people who are not lovable, you must realize that all of them are loved by God. If you do not have the love of God on which to repose when others cut and tear your heart, your life will be sad and disillusioned.

[574

... Of God. Place not your trust in God because of your merits! He loves you despite your unworthiness. It is His love which will make you better rather than your betterment which will make Him love you. Often during the day say: "God loves me, and He is on my side, by my side."   [575

... Possessiveness. Love could become so possessive that it would hardly be conscious of the rights of others: lest love so degenerate into a mutual exchange of egotisms, there must be a constant going out to others, an exteriorization, an increased searching for the formation of an "us." Love of God is inseparable from love of neighbor.   [576

... Power Of. To understand its power, one must realize that love does not mean to have, to own, to possess; but to be had, to be owned, to be possessed. It is not the using of another for the sake of self, but the giving of self in order to help another. For one who lives in isolation, love becomes selfishness.   [577

... Reciprocity. Love is reciprocal; it is received in proportion as it is given.   [578

... Reciprocity. Liking is reciprocal, but love is not necessarily reciprocal. The friends we say we like, like us. But a mother can love a wayward son even though he does not return the affection. God can love us even when we spurn His graces.   [579

... Sacrifice; Penance. Unless there is love, sacrifice and penance will be felt as an evil, but not when love is there.   [580

... Saints. It does not require much time to make us saints; it requires only much love.   [581

... Selfishness. The penalty for selfishness in love is terrific. In egotistical love, the ego, or self, is projected into the other, not to love the other, but to love the self and its pleasures immersed in the other . . . Love then degenerates into an epidermic contact or a mutual exchange of egotisms, where there is external contact like that of billiard balls, but no true affection.   [582

... Service. Love is not a circle circumscribed by the ego; it is more like open arms serving humanity.   [583

... Sex. Sex is replaceable, but love is not, because love is always directed to a particular person.   [584

... Sinful. When a sinful love rules the heart, religion and virtue seem like an outward law bristling with prohibitions; every object it presents is repulsive.   [585

... Social. Love is social, or it ceases to be love.   [586

... **Taken Back.** When love is breathed out to another human heart, it is never meant to be taken back. If it is taken back, it suffocates and poisons us. [587

... **Vision.** Love is a kind of vision; it allows a penetration of the character of another which at times far surpasses knowledge. The lover has a vision of beauty which is denied the one who hates. [588

LUST

... **Avarice.** It is a common psychological experience that those who have given way to lust in youth are often those who sin by avarice in their old age. [589

... **Egotism; Greed.** Of the three, lust, egotism and greed, the first is the easiest for the spirit to master, because its excesses create its emptiness . . . but egotism and greed are very difficult to cure, because they are inflationary sins. [590

LUXURY

... **Poverty.** All intense interest in luxury is a mark of inner poverty. [591

LYING

When anyone accuses us of being a sheepstealer, we smile; but when we are accused of being a liar, we are apt to become angry, for it may be true. [592

· · M · ·

MAN

...Actions. What men do to one another, they do to
Him, whether the act be of kindness or bitterness, and out of
those acts will come our judgment. [593

...Animals. The great difference between an animal
and a man is that an animal can have its desires satisfied but
man cannot. [594

...Anxiety; Fear. Man is standing midway between the
animal and the angel, living in a finite world and aspiring
toward the infinite, moving in time and seeking the eternal,
he is pulled at one moment toward the pleasures of the body
and at another moment to the joys of the spirit . . . this
pull of the old Adam and the beautiful attraction of the new
Adam, this necessity of choice which offers him two roads,
one leading to God and the other away from Him—all this
makes man anxious about his destiny beyond the stars and
fearful of his fall to the depths beneath. [595

...Aspirations. With your feet on earth, you dream of
Heaven; creature of time, you despise it; flower of a day, you
seek to eternalize yourself. Why do you want Life, Truth,

Beauty, Goodness and Justice, unless you were made for them? [596

... **Beast.** Once man believes that he is a beast, then he immediately proceeds to act as one. [597

... **Complexity.** Man, being complex, is always on a seesaw. If unlawful lusts are repressed, there is an exaltation of the spirit. If, on the contrary, the higher things of the spirit are rejected, there is an inordinate expression of lust. [598

... **Creature Of God.** Man is by nature a creature of God, as humbly as a table is a creature of the carpenter; if he suddenly begins to throb with the very life of God, so that he can call God not his Creator but his Father, that is a supernatural act for a man. Man then *becomes* something which he *was* not; that elevation of his nature can come only as a gift from God. [599

... **Dimension.** Formerly, man lived in a three-dimensional universe. On earth which he inhabited with his neighbors, he looked forth to Heaven above and to hell below. Forgetting God, man's vision has lately been reduced to a single dimension; namely, that of his own mind. [600

... **God.** Men of other generations went to God from the order in the universe; the modern man goes to God through the disorder in himself . . . It is the human personality, not nature, which really interests and troubles men today. [601

...God. The spirit of modern philosophy is divinization of man and humanization of God. Stressing his own sufficiency, making himself the measure of Being and Truth, attributing to himself a divine knowledge and a participated Divine nature, man has pulled down God from the heavens and reduced Him to a mere shadow of Himself.   [602

...Good; Evil. Man has aspirations to good which he finds it impossible to realize completely by himself; at the same time, he has an inclination toward evil which solicits him away from these ideals. He is like a man who is down a well through his own stupidity. He knows he ought not to be there, but he cannot get out by himself. Or, to change the picture, he is like a clock whose mainspring is broken. He needs to be fixed on the inside, but the repairs must be supplied from without. He is mistaken if he is an optimist who believes evolution will give him a mainspring, or a pessimist, who believes that nobody can fix him. He is a creature who can run well again, but only if some watchmaker will have the kindness to repair him.   [603

...Limited Horizons. The modern soul has definitely limited its horizons; having negated the eternal destinies, it has even lost its trust in nature, for nature without God is traitorous.   [604

...Love; Women. Man's love is always tied up with his intellect; but for a woman, love is its own reason: "I love you because I love you." A man gives reasons because he compares one woman with another; a woman just prefers. A man sees one peach in a basket of peaches; a woman sees only the one peach.   [605

...Modern. Modern man ... has so long believed that right and wrong were only differences in point of view, that now when evil works itself out in practice he is paralyzed to do anything against it. [606

...Modern. We must make a start with modern man as he is, not as we should like to find him. Because our apologetic literature has missed this point, it is about fifty years behind the times. It leaves the modern soul cold, not because its arguments are unconvincing, but because the modern soul is too confused to grasp them. [607

...Unity With God. Ever since the days of Adam, man has been hiding from God and saying, "God is hard to find." [608

...Vacillation. Modern man is no longer a unity, but a confused bundle of complexes and nerves. There is no single over-all purpose in his life. Such a man projects his own mental confusion to the outside world and concludes that, since he knows no truth, nobody can know it. His own skepticism (which he universalizes into a philosophy of life) throws him back more and more upon those powers lurking in the dark, dark caverns of his unconsciousness. He changes his philosophy as he changes his clothes ... His authority is public opinion; when that shifts, his frustrated soul shifts with it. [609

...Woman. A man may stand for the Justice of God, but a woman stands for His Mercy. [610

154

... **World.** The truly good man feels the world is the way it is because in some way he has not been better.　　[611

MARRIAGE

... **Divorce.** Why should we expect our soldiers to be faithful to their country in the muck and mire, when husbands and wives desert the cause at the first bursting of a shell?　　[612

... **Expectation.** Too many married people expect their partner to give that which only God can give, namely, an eternal ecstasy.　　[613

... **Fidelity.** The unification from the duality of flesh of husband and wife is one of the reasons why the Savior forbade the breaking of the bond. Both men and women, in the moment of the knowing, receive a gift which neither ever knew before, and which they can never know again except by repetition. The resulting psychic changes are as great as the somatic. The woman can never return again to virginity; the man can never return again to ignorance. Something has happened to make them one, and from that oneness come fidelity, so long as either has a body.　　[614

... **Listening.** When an audience goes to hear a concert singer, it does not sing back at the operatic star. In marriage, too, there must be moments of intelligent listening and genuine ir.terest.　　[615

... **Love.** As time goes on, the river of rapture of husband and wife broadens. The eddies of passion may remain in the

155

shallows, but their current never stops flowing. The companionship that began in ecstasies of flesh now widens into the sharing of bread, the communion of mind, and heart, and will, as they taste the sweet delirium of simply being together. Love is soon discovered to be oneness, more than the mere assimilation at which new lovers strain. The glamor passes, but the mystery deepens until they are made one through the deep sharing of life's meaning in the mystery of an eternal love that gave only to receive.   [616

...**Personal.** No one minds eating in public, because there is not a personal union of the food and the stomach. But making love in public is vulgar because, by its very nature, love is personal. It exists between two persons, and only two, and therefore resents intrusion or vulgarity. Their love is spoiled when others know it, and so marriage is spoiled when a third knows its secret.   [617

...**Physical Attraction.** Physical attractiveness has a terrible way of disappearing after marriage. The young man who was admired for strength as he made an end run on a football field one Saturday afternoon seems to lose all vigor when he is asked to take down the screens in the autumn.
[618

...**Physical Love.** Physical love does not continue with the same ecstasy. If flesh is the only medium of married love, then marriage must suffer the penalties of the flesh; transience and death.   [619

...**Problems.** There is a marriage in which the husband may be an alcoholic or the wife a spendthrift, or the husband unfaithful or the wife always nagging, or he is a "beast" or she is "impossible." What is going to be done in a case like that? *Stick it out!* Remain faithful! Why? Suppose the husband, instead of being an alcoholic, had pneumonia. Would the wife nurse him and care for him? If he is a sinner he has moral pneumonia and is spiritually sick; why abandon him? A mother has a child with polio; does she give up the child?

[620

... **Purity.** Purity is a consciousness that each possesses a gift which can be *given* only once, and can be *received* only once. In the unity of flesh he makes her a woman; she makes him a man. They may enjoy the gift many times, but once given it can never be taken back, either in man or in woman. It is not just a physiological experience, but the unraveling of a mystery. As one can pass just once from ignorance to knowledge of a given point, for example, the principle of contradiction, so one can pass just once from incompleteness to the full knowledge of self which the partner brings. Once that border line is crossed, neither belongs wholly to self. Their reciprocity has created dependence; the riddle has been solved, the mystery has been revealed; the dual have become a unity, either sanctioned by God or in defiance of His will.

[621

... **Understanding.** Very few married people ever understand that life is a crisscross pattern; the threads of the fabric go away early in marriage, and during the second crisis they cross in the opposite direction. In the beginning of love, in the sex period, it is dinners, dances, rides, parties, and cocktail hours, which prove the cement of love. Now, in the

157

second stage, the cement is totally different but it is equally real, namely, misfortunes, children, sickness, sorrows, trials, and bereavements. Pleasures do not unite people as much as pain and sorrow can. Soldiers on a battlefield are more closely united than people viewing a scene in a movie theater. [622

... **Unity.** As the Scriptures tell us: "The unbelieving husband is sanctified by the believing wife; and the unbelieving wife is sanctified by the believing husband" (I Corinthians 7:14). This is one of the most forgotten texts on the subject of marriage. It applies to the spiritual order, the common experience of the physical. If a husband is ill, the wife will nurse him back to health. In the spiritual order, the one who has faith and love of God will take on the burdens of the unbeliever, such as drunkenness, infidelity, and mental cruelty, for the sake of his soul. What a blood transfusion is to the body, reparation for the sins of another is to the spirit. Instead of separating when there are difficulties and trials, the Christian solution is to bear the other as a cross for the sake of his sanctification. The wife can redeem the husband, and the husband the wife. [623

MARTYRS

There have been more martyrs, and more Christian blood has been shed in the last 40 years than in the 300 years of the Roman persecution. [624

... **Modern.** Never in history have there been as many martyrs as there are today. The martyrdoms of the first 250 years of Christian history are trivial in comparison to the

unnumbered heroes of the soul who have died for the faith
today.   [625

MARXISM

Marxism is at one and the same time a product of a
bourgeois, liberal civilization and a judgment upon it. Its
protests are just, but its judgments and reforms are wrong,
because it has failed to recognize the privacy of personality.
Its doctrine of opposites is held together by a suicidal inco-
herence, which is a secularization of the Christian idea of
the Kingdom of God, as Hegelianism was the secularization
of the idea of the Trinity. It has tried to solve the problem of
Frustrated Man, but it adds frustration to frustration by
annihilating man's nature and by equating original sin with
private property.   [626

... **Marx, Karl.** Marx had two sources of income. One
briefly came from his services as foreign correspondent for
the *New York Tribune*. The other source of his income was
his rich friend, Friedrich Engels, the son of a merchant in
Manchester ... It is easy to understand how a man who
never earned his own living, but survived through the aid of
others, should so readily develop a system of economics based
on the dispossession of others.   [627

THE MASS

The Mass is the Sacrifice of the Mystical Body of Christ,
and is one with Calvary, which was the sacrifice of the
physical body of Christ. The Mass, in other words, is a
supra-temporal reality, by which the glorified Christ in

Heaven prolongs His sacrifice on the cross by and through us. [628

MATERIALISM

... Individuals. Materialism, denying the supreme worth of the individual, finds him something to be used rather than respected. [629

... Souls. The richer the soul, the less store it sets on the material. [630

... Symbolism. The first effect of materialism is to be seen in architecture which is devoid of all ornamentation. When a civilization has faith, matter is used to symbolize the spirit; hence such decorations as gargoyles, phoenixes, wheat, and grapes. When a civilization ceases to believe in the spirit, then there is nothing to represent symbolically. [631

... Values. There seems to be no place for values except the material. Perhaps a more correct way to put it would be that values have disappeared and sensations have taken their place. [632

MEDIOCRITY

The world loves the mediocre. The world hates the very good and the very bad. The good are a reproach to the mediocre, and the evil are a disturbance. That is why Christ was crucified with thieves. [633

... Calvary. Calvary was the price He paid for the Sermon on the Mount. Only mediocrity survives. Those who call black black and white white are sentenced for intolerance. Only the grays live. [634

MEDITATION

Meditation is a more advanced spiritual act than "saying prayers." It may be likened to the attitude of a child who breaks into the presence of a mother saying: "I'll not say a word, if you will just let me stay here and watch you." Or, as a soldier once told the Curé of Ars: "I just stand here before the tabernacle; He looks at me and I look at Him." [635

... Listening. For meditation the ear of the soul is more important than the tongue: St. Paul tells us that faith comes from listening. [636

... Results Of. If a man meditates consistently on God, a complete revolution takes place in his behavior. If in a morning meditation he remembers how God became a humble servant of man, he will not lord it over others during the day. If there were a meditation of His redemption of all men, he would cease to be a snob. Since our Lord took the world's sins upon Himself, the man who has dwelt on this truth will seek to take up the burdens of his neighbor, even though they were not of his making—for the sins the Lord bore were not of His making, either. If the meditation stressed the merciful Savior Who forgave those who crucified Him, so a man will forgive those who injure him, that he may be worthy of forgiveness. These thoughts do not come from ourselves—for we are incapable of them—nor from the world—for they are unworldly thoughts. They come from God alone. [637

. . . Results Of. When one meditates and fills his mind for an hour a day with thoughts and resolutions bearing on the love of God and neighbor above all things, there is a gradual seepage of love down to the level of what is called the subconscious, and finally these good thoughts emerge, of themselves, in the form of effortless good actions. Everyone has verified in his own life a thousand times the ideomotor character of thought. [638

. . . Time For. It is never true to say that we have no time to meditate; the less one thinks of God, the less time there will always be for Him. [639

MEEKNESS

A weak man can never be meek, because he is never self-possessed; meekness is that virtue which controls the combative, violent and pugnacious powers of our nature, and is therefore the best and noblest road to self-realization. [640

MELANCHOLY

The striking of the breast when there is abandonment of redemptive hope can sometimes mean a beating out of one's own life, in a slow suicide. The melancholic without a world view concentrates on death and lives in a kind of anticipated death. [641

Melancholy is something so deep in our modern mood that its analysis should not be committed solely to the psychiatrist. It is not simply a disgust, or discontent, or sorrow, or even a suffering. In suffering, the emphasis is generally on external things and circumstances which make one sad; in

melancholy, there is something interior which has been
wounded, there is a kind of discontent of self, a hatred of
being, a desire to be empty. [642

MEMORY

... Conscience. Since memory contains the material on
which our conscience passes judgment, it follows that the
best way to rid ourselves of bad memory is to cleanse consciences. Then the record which was once a shame begins to
be our glory. Since it is a fact that the more displeasing
certain things are, the more apt they are to be recalled, may
not this be an evidence of the mercy of God, who shows us
the wound, that we can call Him in as Physician of our
souls? [643

MENTAL HEALTH

... Conscience. Nothing helps good mental health as
much as a good conscience. [644

MERCY

... Judgment. If on the last day we would receive a
merciful judgment, we must begin here below to be merciful
to others. Just as the clouds release only the moisture which
they gathered from the earth, so too can Heaven release only
the mercy we have sent heavenward. [645

MILITARISM

The rise of militarism and the Gospel of Force in the
modern world is a result of the vacuum created by the
abandonment of the Cross. [646

MIND

...**Neglected.** The garden left uncultivated becomes full of weeds. A neglected mind runs into feebleness and ignorance. If we do not aspire to that which is higher, we revert to that which is lower. [647

...**Open.** The open mind is commendable when it is open like a road that leads to a city which is its destination. But the open mind is condemnable when it is like an abyss or a manhole. [648

...**Problems.** In other generations, the mind had problems; the mind of today *is* a problem. [649

...**Receptiveness.** The relation between a teacher and a student, or the relation between a truth and a mind is not like a glove to a hand; it is rather like the body to medicine. Bodies that are whole and normal co-operate with the medicine, it is not the pill alone that cures a patient; the pill would be as useless in a stomach as on a table if there were not a potency and a capacity in the body which makes it capable of assimilating the cure. So it is with the mind; not everyone accepts a truth as a clean window receives light. [650

MISSIONS

...**Need.** May the Holy Spirit teach us that the world is on our back as the Cross was on the back of Christ. Christ did not die for our parish or our dioceses. He died for ALL mankind. [651

. . . Propagation. God is dead in a parish that spends millions and millions on a church and never gives one one-hundreth of that to propagate the faith in Asia or Africa. God is dead in all those who restrict their religion to prayers and church attendance and do not live out the incarnation, loving all men for whom Christ died.   [652

MODERN AGE

The Puritans introduced thrift into the American way of life. The Puritan way was to save first, then enjoy. The modern way is to go to Europe now, pay later. Colonial Americans decreased their wants in order to increase their security. Contemporary Americans increase their wants in the hope that the state may insure their security.   [653

MODERN SOCIETY

. . . Money. Modern Society is what might be characterized as acquisitive . . . its aristocracy is not one of blood or virtue, but of money . . . Our Blessed Lord came into the world to destroy this acquisitiveness . . . It is worth noting immediately that "the poor in spirit" does not necessarily mean the indigent or those in straitened circumstances of life. "Poor in Spirit" means interior detachment, and as such includes even some who are rich in the world's goods, for detachment can be practiced by the rich just as avarice can be practiced by the poor.   [654

MODERN THEOLOGY

In the parable of the soil and the seed, our dear Lord likened some minds to the seed that fell among thorns. They received the grace, but there was a parallel growth of seed and thorns, of faith and underbrush, of intellectuality and superficiality, of sacramental regeneration and "Pepsi-generation," Magazine theology and protest banner, the City of God and the Secular City. Then, when the first catastrophe comes, the first challenge to their ego, the first splinter from the cross, they leave this "new theology" for they are Christians who give Christ their finger, but refuse to give their hand.   [655

MONEY

Money, like grace, is to be kept in circulation. It is like seed: it is good for nothing in a heap; it does good only when it is spread around.   [656

... **Leisure.** One of the greatest deceptions of today is the belief that leisure and money are the two essentials of happiness. The sad fact of life is that there are no more frustrated people on the face of the earth than those who have nothing to do and those who have too much money for their own good.   [657

MORALITY

The masses of people are generally inclined to equate morality with the general level of society at any given moment. Numbers become the measure of goodness. If a sufficient number can be counted who violate a certain Commandment of God, then it is argued: "Fifty million adulterers cannot be wrong. We have to change the Commandments."   [658

... **Modern.** Modern man is naked. He has been stripped by false prophets who told him that his old clothes of morality were out of date. Now, none of the new suits he puts on can cover his nakedness; moreover, they give him considerable discomfort. [659

... **Subhuman.** We are scandalized at seeing what the release of the subhuman has done to the Fascists, Nazis, and Communists. Yet we have not learned that the same deleterious effects can be present in the individual who, starting with the philosophy that he is only a beast, immediately proceeds to act like one. To just the extent that a man is unmortified in his selfish passions, it becomes necessary for some external authority to control and subdue those passions. That is why the passing of morality and religion and asceticism from political life is inevitably followed by a police state, which attempts to organize the chaos produced by that selfishness. [660

MOTHERHOOD

Every mother, when she picks up the young life that has been born to her, looks up to the heavens to thank God for the gift which made the world young again. [661

In lower forms of life, such as the amoeba, there is a fission, or splitting, as the young life breaks off from the parent cell. Motherhood is still a long way off, for there could never be a mother without an intimate, close, and vital relationship between the body of the mother and the body of the young offspring . . . Some land crabs come down from the mountains to the sea, push their eggs into the water, and then abandon them. No real motherhood here, for the young never see their mother nor do the mothers care for the young . . . As we see nature unfold, there is an increasing unity of mother and offspring until finally many mothers carry the young within them. Despite all this . . . there could never be a human mother until love came into the world . . . In addition to sex, which is common to the animals, there must also be love, in order that there be no ravishing or stealing away of the worth of the person. If a mother is to be made, then what is begotten must come from a free act of the will, in which a woman freely submits to the love of a man . . . One might almost say that the generation begins in the mind and in the soul with love and completes itself in the body . . . Mothers in the animal kingdom care only for a body; mothers in the spiritual kingdom must care also for a soul, a mind, and a heart.   [662

MOTHERS

The mother is both the physical preserver of life and the moral provider of truth; she is nature's constant challenge to death, the bearer of cosmic plenitude, the herald of eternal realities, God's great cooperator.   [663

. . . Beauty.   If any one of us could have made our own mother, we would have made her the most beautiful woman in the world.   [664

. . . Child's Faith.   The cogency of the child's faith is not based on the sum of reasons leading up to it, but on the weight of the mother's authority, who would not deceive.   [665

. . . Fathers.   The mother is the court of equity in the home; the father is the court of law. The mother reveals that other attribute of Divinity—which is mercy, love, and forgiveness. When the mother threatens, "I will tell your father," the child will often beg her to keep secret his failure, that he may enjoy her mercy.   [666

... Sons. On one occasion, Whistler was complimented for the beautiful painting of his mother. His answer was, "You know how it is. One tries to make one's Mommy as nice as one can." There is no reason to feel that Christ would do otherwise, for, as God, He preexisted His Own Mother.
[667

MOTIVATION

Man is motivated by an urge, an unquenchable desire to enlarge his vision and to know the ultimate meaning of things.   [668

MUSIC

... Kinds Of. There are various kinds of music: there is head music, such as the music of Bach; there is heart music, like Schubert's; and then there is what might be called visceral music, that is, music which stirs legs, arms, and the body in general.   [669

NATIONS

... **Moral Failure.** Nations, too, can get in the habit of denying that their trials, the hatred of other nations, their insecurity, and the threat of Communism may be related to their moral failings. It is too superficial a justification for any nation to blame another for its crises. [670

NATURE

... **Man.** Nature follows the path of least resistance; that is why all rivers are crooked. But human nature constructs obstacles in order to perfect itself. In all games there are boundaries and rules and hurdles which intensify the sport. A deed is praised because it is difficult. Golf must have its traps and its rough; otherwise the game would be without interest. [671

NEGLECT

To neglect one's vocation in idleness, regardless of the intensity of the miscarried work, is serious. Today's neglect cannot be performed tomorrow without neglecting tomorrow's work. [672

We can lose our souls, not only by doing evil, but also by neglecting the good. [673

NEGLIGENCE

Not to use a power is wrong. To withhold help is to participate in the authorship of misery that we fail to relieve. Violence slays thousands, but supine negligence slays millions. [674

NEIGHBORS

... Borrowing. There is probably less borrowing of sugar in all of the apartments of New York City than there is in a village of five hundred. [675

... Definition. The neighbor is not the one next door. The neighbor is the one in need, or may be even an enemy. [676

... Love. If people only knew how happy they would make themselves if they really helped their neighbor for the love of God, we would soon become a nation with songs in our hearts, as well as on our lips. [677

NEUROSIS

... Cause. Many of the compulsion neuroses in our modern world are due to the same cause: a fear of punishment due to some deep, unabsolved sense of guilt. People dread what they deserve, but having denied their sin, they punish themselves instead of seeking the mercy of God. [678

NEUROTICS

We need not predicate a universal suppressed desire for incest to explain why many clients develop a deep dependence on their analysts. Almost every neurotic wants attention. He is preoccupied with himself and fearful of failure. It is no wonder, when he finds an analyst or psychotherapist who is willing to listen—whose task it is to listen—that this person begins to play a great role in the patient's life.   [679

NON-ATTACHMENT

We cannot say, with Aldous Huxley, "The ideal man is the non-attached man. Non-attached to his bodily sensations and lusts. Non-attached to his cravings for power and possessions. Non-attached even to science and speculation and philanthropy." The non attachment of Buddhism or Taoism is not the Christian ideal; though it sounds very noble to say that they who possess are possessed, are slaves to the illusions of life. Non attachment and unworldliness are vain unless they are regarded as secondary, as a mere means to attain the primary goal, which is love of God and neighbor.   [680

NOTHINGNESS

... **Man.**   Man came from nothingness but he was not made for it. Sartre just put nothingness on the wrong end.
[681

... **Universe.**   If absolute nothingness ever were, then nothing would ever be. Out of the void of nothingness this universe could never come.   [682

OBEDIENCE

Obedience does not mean the execution of orders that are given by a drill sergeant. It springs, rather, from the love of an order, and love of Him who gave it. [683

... **Military; Civil.** Why do we in time of war commend the soldier for obedience to his orders, for his oath of fealty, for fulfillment of his missions, and then in time of peace have such little respect for that same obedience to authority that we outlaw it from our home and schools and produce a race of juvenile delinquents? [684

... **Servility.** Obedience is servility only to those who have not understood the spontaneity of love. [685

OBSCENITY

Obscenity is the turning of mystery into a jest. It is the making of something holy, unholy, and something personal, vulgar. [686

OBSCURITY

Obscurity is a menace only to those who want the plaudits of men. [687

OPEN-MINDNESS

Those who boast of their open-mindness are invariably those who love to search for truth but not to find it; . . . they go through life talking about 'widening the horizons of truth' but without ever seeing the sun.   [688

OPINION

. . . **Race; Class.**   There is too often a tendency to condemn any opinion of a group or a race or class, simply because it belongs to them. A spirit of charity would suggest a willingness to search for the truth in their position, or at least to give it as kindly an interpretation as possible.   [689

ORIGINALITY

. . . **Novelty.**   Novelty and originality are unfortunately too often identified as the same.   [690

··P··

PAGANISM

The pagan fears the loss of his body and his wealth; the
faithful fears the loss of his soul. The believer fears God
with a filial fear such as a devoted son has toward a loving
father; the pagan fears, not God, but his fellow man, who
seems to threaten him. Hence the increase in cynicism,
suspicion, irreverence, strifes, and war; the neighbor must be
killed, by word if not by sword, because he is an enemy to be
dreaded.   [691

PAGANS

... **Christians.** Picture a child with a ball, and suppose
that he is told that it is the only ball he will ever have to play
with. The natural psychological reaction of the child will be
to be fearful of playing too much with it, or bouncing it too
often, or even pricking it full of pin holes, because he will
never have another ball. But suppose that the child is told
that perhaps next month, perhaps next week, perhaps even
in five minutes, he will be given another ball, which will
never wear out, which will always give joy and with which
he will never tire of playing. The natural reaction of the
child will be to take the first ball a little less seriously, and to

175

begin playing with it joyously and happily, not even caring if someone does prick it full of pin holes, because he is very soon going to have another ball which will endure eternally. The child with one ball is the modern pagan who has only one ball in the sense that he has one sphere, one world, one life, one earth. He cannot enjoy the earth as much as he would like because he must always be fearful of the earth being taken away from him. He can never even tolerate that any suffering or pain should ever come to his little ball, the earth, for it is the only ball that he will ever have to play with. The Christian, on the other hand, is the one who believes that some day, perhaps even tomorrow, he will have another ball, another world, another sphere, another life. And so he can begin to play with this earth, enjoy its monotony, and even be resigned to its pinpricks, for he knows that very soon he is going to have the other ball, which is the other life that will never wear out nor become tiresome, because its life is the life of the eternal God, the beginning and the end of all that is. [692

PAIN

Pain in itself is not unbearable; it is the failure to understand its meaning that is unbearable. [693

... **Capacity.** Our capacity for pain is greater than our capacity for pleasure. Suffering reaches the point where we feel we can endure it no longer, and yet it increases and we endure it . . . Our capacity for pain is greater because the Good Lord intended that all pain should be exhausted in this world. The Divine Plan is to have real joys in the next life. [694

... **Salvation.** All of you, therefore, who for months and years have lain crucified on beds of pain, remember that an hour will come when you will be taken down from your cross, and the Savior shall look upon your hands and feet and sides to find there the imprint of His wounds which will be your passport to eternal joy; for being made like Him in His death, you shall be made like Him in His glory. [695

... **Solutions.** There are actually three solutions about pain. One is the Stoic solution, which is to grit your teeth and bear it. The second is the Buddhist, which holds that all pain and suffering come from desire. If we could extinguish all our desires, we would eventually reach a point of tranquillity where we would be absorbed into the great Nirvana of unconsciousness. The third solution is the Hebraic-Christian philosophy of pain, which believes that pain and suffering can be transcended. [696

PARENTS

... **Discipline.** Mothers who are afraid to discipline think pain is more serious than wrong. When children grow up, they will not dislike their parents because they disciplined them when wrong, but because they never gave them a moral sense of right and wrong. [697

... **Guidance.** Parents were once teen-agers and hence know the strength and weakness of those difficult years. Parents have greater vision and are capable of better guidance than youth suspects. [698

... **Perfection.** To every child, parents are the mirrors of

177

perfection; the father is the strongest, the mother is the nicest. The two images in some way confound and reveal the sovereign justice and the merciful goodness of God.   [699

... **Permissiveness.**   It is the parents who allow their children to do everything they please who are not loved later on in life.   [700

... **Standards.**   The great tragedy today is that parents themselves are so often without any convincing standards to offer for the guidance of their children. They have the sextant but no fixed star, the technique but no destiny, the material but no blueprints, the means but no ends.   [701

PASSION
... **Sanctity.**   Strong passions are the precious raw material of sanctity. Individuals who have carried their sinning to extremes should not despair or say, "I am too great a sinner to change," or "God would not want *me*." God will take anyone who is willing to love, not with an occasional gesture, but with a "passionless passion," a "wild tranquillity." A sinner, unrepentant, cannot love God, any more than a man on dry land can swim; but as soon as he takes his errant energies to God and asks for their redirection, he will become happy, as he was never happy before. It is not the wrong things one has already done which keep one from God; it is present persistence in that wrong.   [702

PAST
Modern man is alienating himself from the past under the false assumption that nothing that was ever thought before or done before is worth preserving.   [703

We owe a greater debt to the past than is generally recognized. The waters of ancient cultures are constantly washing our shores. [704

PATRIOTISM

... **Soldiers.** Who does the most to preserve patriotism in a nation? It is not the politicians who talk about duties; it is not the dramatist who glorifies its past. The ideals of patriotism in a nation are best preserved by soldiers on the battlefield who are prepared to die. [705

PEACE

Peace is not a passive, but an active virtue. [706

... **Christ.** When Chile and Argentina were about to go to war, it was the suggestion of a woman that the cannons of the two nations be melted, made into a statue of Christ and placed in the Andes at the border of each and be called "The Christ of the Andes." And it bears this inscription: "Sooner shall these mountains crumble than this pact of peace, entered into at the feet of Christ between these two nations, shall be broken." And that pact has never been broken! [707

... **Definition.** The best definition of peace ever given came from the pen of St. Augustine: "Peace is the tranquillity of order." It is not tranquillity alone, for thieves can be tranquil in the possession of their spoils; rather it is the tranquillity of order; order implies justice . . . peace is the fruit of justice. [708

... **Godlessness.** If true peace is to be won, it must first be won in our own hearts. Let us turn back to God and establish justice in our souls. Russia will perish because it is anti-God; but we shall not survive if in the face of Communism we are Godless. [709

... **Justice.** Peace is inseparable from justice. One does not really set out to have peace; peace is a by-product of justice. [710

... **Love.** Peace is a fruit of love, and love flowers in the man oriented toward God. The greatest privilege that can come to man is to have his life God-directed; this follows when he has remotely paved the way by disciplined self-direction. God cares enough for us to regulate our lives—and this is the strongest proof of love that He could give us. For it is a fact of human experience that we do not care very much about the details of other people's lives unless we love them. We are not deeply interested in hearing more of those individuals whom we meet in the subway and in the street and on the highway. But as soon as we begin to know and love any of them, then we become more and more interested in their lives; we have a greater care for them. As we bring them into the area of our love, both our interest and their happiness increases. It is like this when we bring ourselves into the area of God's love: there is an increasing Divine guidance of the details of our life, and we are ever being made more sure of the depth and reality of His Love. To the extent that we abandon our personality to Him, He will take possession of our will and work in us. We are no longer ruled by commands coming from the outside, as from a cruel master, but by almost imperceptible suggestions that rise up from within. We feel as if we had wanted all along to do those things He suggests to us; we are never conscious of being under command. Thus our service to Him becomes the highest form of liberty, for it is always easy to do something for the one we love.   [711

... Soviet. What do the Soviets mean by peace? Peace to them means any condition or state of affairs of the world in which the Soviets are allowed to do whatever they please.   [712

... War. Peace is made only by war—war not against others but against sin and selfishness and egotism; war is waged with the Cross, not one that fights outward like Peter's sword, which cuts off the ears of others, but rather a sword that is thrust inward to cut out selfishness that destroys the brotherhood of man under the Fatherhood of God and the Redemption of His Divine Son. God hates peace in those who are destined for war, and we are all destined for war against that which is base and rotten in ourselves.   [713

... Win or Purchase. Ruskin has warned us that peace may be either *bought* or it may be *won*. It is won by resistance to evil; it is bought by compromise with evil.   [714

PEACE OF SOUL

There is a world of difference between peace of mind and peace of soul . . . The peaceful soul does not seek, now, to live morally, but to live for God; morality is only a by-product of the union with Him.   [715

PENANCE

Penances are not done by ourselves alone; the penitent is helped by others who are in the Body of Christ. This could not be if we were isolated individuals, but it can come about if we belong to one Mystical Body where all are one because governed by one Head, vivified by one Soul, and professing the same Faith. [716

PENTECOST

If God can communicate His Power to a human nature made one with His Divine Person in the Incarnation, why can not He continue to communicate it through other human natures made one with Him be the unifying spirit of Pentecost? [717

PERFECTION

Our Blessed Lord suggested that we be satisfied with nothing less than perfection: 'Be ye perfect as your Heavenly Father is perfect.' This does not mean that we are to be perfect as God is perfect, but to be perfect in a Godlike and not a human way. What is startling about this command is that we are bidden not to imitate others, but God. [718

... Man. Whenever anyone hears of a new psychological theory such as the ability to see the future in a dim way, or reads of a drug which retards old age, there is almost a cosmic rush to the conclusion that in a few years humanity will be free from error and immune from disease. This urge to perfection is right and good, for there is no reason why the evolutionary process should stand still once it comes to man. But the fallacy is that man always thinks of this perfection as coming to him without his own effort or the exercise of his own will . . . perfection is thus taken out of the moral order and reduced to the physical order; it is something that is given to us, rather than something we acquire; it comes like a surprise legacy which we did not earn nor merit, rather than as a prize which was won by blood and sweat and tears. The truth is that perfection has something to do with becoming what we are not, and that this becoming is achieved through willing, self-discipline and even suffering, and implies an ideal above us and one toward which we strive. [719

PERSECUTION

... **Result Of.** One great and mysterious fact that is not generally known to the world is that wherever there is persecution on account of the Faith, it always results in a vast catch of souls for the Kingdom of God. Tertullian was right when he said: "Blood of the Martyrs is the seed of the Church." [720

PERSON

... **Abnormal.** The abnormal person is to be likened to a radio which is tuned into several stations simultaneously and which receives nothing but annoying static. He is no longer a unit, but a confused bundle of complexes and nerves, a kind of menagerie in which a number of beasts each seeks its own prey. [721

PERSONALITY

... **Abnormal.** Personality, to the abnormal, is nothing but the product of instinctive desires and impulses. Reason dances to the tunes piped for it by instincts. Judgments are, to the abnormal, so many attempts to prop up illusions with arguments. Reason and will are only corks bobbing up and down on the waves of unconsciousness and are determined by the currents below the surface. [722

PETER

He says to them: "And what of you? Who do you say that I am?" . . . And the twelve Apostles do not answer. Then something happens which is less of man than of God. One man now steps forward. It is he who is always mentioned first in every list of the Apostles. He is named one hundred and ninety-five times in the Gospels, while all the other Apostles together are mentioned only one hundred and thirty times. He is the only person, outside of His heavenly Father, whom Our Lord so united to Himself as to say: "We." He is also the third man in history whose name is changed by God . . . This same man whose name was changed to Rock now steps forward, not because the Apostles asked him to do so, not because he was smarter than the others, or because he knew the answer in his own flesh and blood, but because there came to him a great light, a light that made him first for eternity. That heavenly revelation gave him the answer to the question of the Master as with infallible certitude he affirmed: "Thou art the Christ, the Son of the Living God." [723

PHILOSOPHERS

. . . Bergson. M. Bergson, the inspiration of modern philosophy, after writing three volumes on the philosophy of becoming, finally confesses that the Aristotelian doctrine is really "the natural metaphysics of the human mind," which, however, he condemns. [724

184

...Berkeley. Berkeley, the English Empirical Idealist, refuted his whole philosophy by dodging a runaway horse. [725

...Chesterton. Mr. Chesterton upsets the extreme determinist philosopher by asking him why he says "thank you" for the mustard. [726

...Schopenhauer. Schopenhauer nullified his philosophy of cosmic suicide by dying a natural death. [727

PHILOSOPHY

...Justification. Most people justify the way they live; that is to say, instead of fitting their lives to a philosophy, they invent a philosophy to fit their lives. [728

...Man. In happier days, philosophers discussed the problem of man; now they discuss man as a problem. [729

...Reason. Eventually philosophy grows desperate and tired from trying to fit a particular age and therefore never pleasing the ages, and is prepared to reject reason altogether. Rationalism fades into irrationalism. Dadaism in art becomes Dadaism in philosophy, as minds in their antipathy to reason seek to escape into absolute spontaneity and license. The dark, subconscious mental confusions are thrown onto canvass as a more genuine portrayal of self than the conclusions of reason. Surrealism enthrones the psychopathic irrationalist; dream worlds are substitutes for thought worlds. Music, too, glorifies motion. Dissonance becomes a goal in itself as

an evidence of the protest against ends, purposes, and reason.
[730

... **Self-Denial.** It is not easy to say "No" to oneself. That is why so many philosophers have erected a philosophy of life based on saying "Yes" to every impulse and desire while dignifying it with the name "self-expression." [731

PLEASURE

... **Love.** Love that always seems to seek its own pleasure is never really satisfied with the love that it gets. What often was the "ideal woman" or the "ideal man" at the beginning becomes "a bore" within eighteen months. [732

POLITICS

... **Conflict.** The conflict of the future will be between a God religion and a state religion, between Christ and antichrist, but in political disguise. [733

... **Material.** Politics has become so all-possessive of life, that by impertinence it thinks that the only philosophy a man can hold is the *right* or the *left*. Had we eyes less material, we would see that there are two other directions where a man with a soul may look—*up* or *down*. [734

... **Religion.** There are two contradictory charges against religion today—the first is that religion is not political enough; the other is that religion is too political. On the one hand the Church is blamed for being too divine, and on the other for not being divine enough. It is hated because it is too heavenly, and hated because it is too earthly. Particularly significant it is that these were the very two charges for which our Lord Himself was condemned—the religious judges Annas and Caiphas found Him too religious; the political judges, Pilate and Herod, found Him too political.

[735

... **The Church.** The Church does not interfere in politics. If by interference in politics is meant judging or condemning a philosophy of life which makes the party, or the state, or the class, or the race the source of all rights, and which usurps the soul and enthrones party over conscience, the answer is emphatically "Yes." The church does judge such a philosophy. But when it does this, it is not interfering with politics, for such politics is no longer politics but a kind of religion that is antireligious.

[736

POOR

... **Hospitality.** The poor cannot reward us for hospitality; therefore God will have to do so. It was these He asked us to invite to our dinners, and it is interesting to note that He always called them, not a meal but a "banquet."

[737

POPULARITY

Popularity is like bloom on a cheek. A bloom is the effect of health. So popularity is to be the by-product of a work well done or the faithful performance of duty. When popularity is artificially stimulated, it is very much like rouge on a cheek.

[738

PORNOGRAPHY

Recently there was held a United Nations Congress on the prevention of crime. It is strange to say that no one spoke

187

out more strongly against all pornographic, horror publications and immoral literature than did L. N. Smirnov of the Soviet Union. He dealt with those who contend that to restrain immoral literature is to curtail freedom, saying: "Talking about human rights in connection with putting this degrading matter before juveniles is like the devil quoting the Bible." [739

POSSESSIVENESS

... **Spirit.** The body may be owned, but the spirit cannot be owned any more than we can clutch the winds in our fists. [740

POVERTY

... **Slums.** We leave our churches each Sunday after witnessing Calvary in the Mass, unbruised and unscarred. That is why we do not worry about the wrecks of humanity—our brothers in Christ, the slum dwellers who are not finding God, because they cannot believe that we believe Christ wants us to love them. [741

... **Spiritual.** Poverty is basically not an economic problem, but a spiritual problem. [742

... **The Poor.** We are living in a new age where holiness will be inseparable from the service of impoverished humanity . . . He who professes to love God and not the poor, does not love God, Who became poor for our sakes that we might become rich. [743

... **Wealth.** Once a self-made man gets a drink inside of him, he begins a conversation with: "Let me tell you how I started as a poor boy. I didn't have a cent." The only time they begin to appreciate poverty is when they begin to be rich. [744

POWER

... **Love.** A person who turns on an electric switch in the house may live under the illusion that he himself has caused the light which is in the room, but actually at a great distance is a dynamo which supplies the electricity. We do not create but merely utilize the power. When one person falls in love with another, he is merely turning on the switch that releases the tremendous reservoir of love which has its source in the Infinite. One heart, one flower, one sunset ought to be enough to satisfy the human heart if it were made only for this world; but the constant search for the "more" is an indication that we were made for something greater than any love we find on this earth. [745

PRAGMATISM

... **Marxism.** Pragmatism and Marxism ignore the memory of the human race, either because the only thing that matters is the useful, or because the good of former times is regarded as anti-revolutionary. [746

PRAYER

All we need do is to voice these two petitions: Dear Lord, illumine my intellect to see the Truth, and give me the strength to follow it. It is a prayer that is *always* answered . . . it makes no difference whether the desire for God we voice has come from our disgusts, satieties, and despair or whether it is born of our love of the beautiful, the perfect.

God is willing to take either our old bones or our young dreams, for He loves us, not because of the way we are, but because of what we can be through His grace.   [747

...**Answers.** When people complain that their prayers are not heard by God, what often has happened is that they did not wait to hear His answer.   [748

...**Answers.** How can God answer the prayers we address to Him unless we answer the prayers others address to us? Do we answer the prayers of the poor? the maimed? the lame? the sinner? the missionary? If not, then by what right can we expect God to answer our requests?   [749

...**Christ.** In the Gospel there are fifteen mentions of the prayers of Our Lord, and most of them were offered in the silence of the desert, or very early in the morning, or on the mountaintops.   [750

...**Essence.** The essence of prayer is not the effort to make God give us something . . . Rather, the purpose of prayer is to give Him the opportunity to bestow the gifts He will give us when we are ready to accept them.   [751

...**Knowing God.** If you want to know about God, there is only one way to do it: get down on your knees. [752

...**Marriage.** If the young couple can pray together, it means that they have the same sense of right and wrong, which is essential for happiness. Nothing makes courtesy and charm as much as conscience. If there are prayers together, then the love of husband and wife will not be directed to one another as an object, but rather both will point as arrows to the Infinite outside of them . . . Prayer will avoid that disillusionment in which one may say to the other, "I sought of thee a soul; I found only a body." He who is not spiritual in the flesh will become carnal in soul.　　[753

. . . **Schools.** I would suggest that the prayer that be said in all of the schools of this country be the prayer that every member of Congress is already carrying with him in his pocket: "In God we trust." I think that prayer is sufficient. It is already on the seal of the United States, it is already in our traditions, and it is a perfect prayer.　　[754

. . . **Selfish.** Many souls want God to do *their* will; they bring their completed plans and ask Him to rubber-stamp them without a change. The petition of the "Our Father" is changed by them to read: "*My* will be done on earth."　[755

. . . **Types.** The man who thinks only of himself says only prayers of petition; he who thinks of his neighbor says prayers of intercession; he who thinks only of loving and serving God, says prayers of abandonment to God's will, and this is the prayer of the saints.　　[756

PREPAREDNESS
General MacArthur once said he could not win a battle if he had not preceded it with at least one hour's thought . . . Napoleon once spoke of the "post-midnight presence of mind," that is, the interval of calm and thought between moments of intense activity.　　[757

PRESENT

...**Past.** Our present is but the harvest of the past. [758

PRIDE

The higher a steeple rises in the heavens the smaller it becomes; the closer a saint gets to God the less he is in his own eyes. [759

It is a spiritual and a psychological fact that some people who pride themselves on their virtue resent sinners mending their ways. [760

...**Criticism.** People who are very proud often have many things wrong with them on the inside, such as selfishness and conceit. As a result their conscience bothers them, because of their submerged guilt, which they refuse to face. Instead of criticizing themselves, which they ought to do, they project the criticism to others. They reform others instead of themselves, point out the mote in the eye of others without seeing the beam in their own. [761

...**Cynics.** The cynic and the scoffer are common examples of modern pride. They do not pretend to share the knowledge of the learned man; they simply tell us that his knowledge is untrue, that the great disciplines of the mind are a tangle of outworn absurdities, that nothing is worth learning because everything is obsolete. The ignorant man, boasting of his ignorance, thus tries to establish himself as the superior of all those who know more than he: for he knows what they do not know—that study "is a waste of time." [762

...Docility. Pride kills docility and makes a man incapable of ever being helped by God. [763

...Humility. Many minds today will not accept Revelation or faith because their pride has blocked the inflow of new knowledge. Only docile minds can receive new truth. Pride makes a person insoluble and, therefore, prevents his entering into amalgamation with others. Humility, on the contrary, because of its basic receptivity to the good of others, makes it possible to receive the joys of union with God. That is why Our Divine Lord suggested that university professors will have to become children to enter the Kingdom of Heaven. [764

...Humility. The proud man counts his newspaper clippings—the humble man his blessings. [765

...Man; God. Pride is at its peak when man cuts himself off from any relation to God and thus makes himself god. He elevates his relative character into an absolute, very much like a carbon copy calling itself the original. [766

PRIESTLY CELIBACY

The priest is pledged to celibacy, not because human generation is wrong, but because it must yield so that he can devote himself wholly to a higher form of generation: the begetting of children in Christ by bringing to Him those who never knew Him, by restoring to Him those lost in sin, and by arousing in those who already love Christ the inspiration to serve Him more fully as religious or priests. The energy which otherwise would be used for the service of the flesh is not buried in a napkin. It is transformed so that it serves chaste generation in the Spirit. [767

Too often the vow of chastity is presented negatively as the avoiding of carnal and sinful pleasures. But is pure water only the absence of dirt, a white diamond merely the negation of carbon? Chastity is sometimes mistakenly called cold, but not by Francis Thompson, who proclaims it a "passionless passion, a wild tranquillity." Chastity is fire. No life is produced without fire. Even the virginal conception of Our Lady had its fire—not human indeed, but the Fire of the Holy Spirit. At that moment, she undoubtedly had an ecstasy of soul surpassing the flesh ecstasy of all humans combined. Such is the joy of begetting through the Pure Love of the Spirit. [768

PRIESTS

... **Preaching.** The priest who has not kept near the fires of the tabernacle can strike no sparks from the pulpit. [769

... **Priesthood.** Our priesthood is best illumined in the fires of victimhood. We become significant to our fellowmen not by being a regular guy, but by being another Christ. [770

PROCREATION

The disgust that follows from the profanation of the mystery (of purity) is a summons to return to reverence for mystery; it is also a realization that in vain will he snare the music of love who breaks the lute. [771

PROFESSORS

Some professors are nothing but textbooks wired for sound . . . The false assumption of these professors is that education is like the transfusion of blood and that ideas can be poured into the student simply by reading to him, as blood is poured into anemic patients.   [772

. . . **Morals; Religion.** Whenever a professor attacks morality and makes fun of religion before his pupils, you can be sure nine times out of ten that his life is rotten.   [773

PROFIT-SHARING

. . . **Corporations; Employees.** In corporations there ought to be some form of co-ownership in which a worker would receive some part of the profits which he has helped to produce . . . Stockholders often are not interested in this suggestion, because they believe that it would mean a decrease in their returns, forgetful that there will be greater increase if those who labor also share in the management. Some labor leaders do not like it, because it decreases the tension between capital and labor. Marxists will not like it because they want the whole industry to be in the hands of the Party leaders. Each of these groups fear for their privileged possession, but the workers themselves will like it because then they will be working not *for* someone, but *with* someone.   [774

PROGRESS

. . . **Goals.** Sometimes, of course, it is not always easy to see just how much progress we are making toward our goal, but though we never see the progress, we never lose sight of the goal. Then we are very much like the tapestry workers, who work not from the front of the tapestry, but always from the rear, keeping ever before their eyes the model of the work to be achieved. They go on drawing thread after thread in a monotonous but thrilling way, never destined to see their completed work until the last thread has been drawn, and the tapestry is turned about to show them how well and how truly they have labored.   [775

... **Pride; Humanity.**   The humble man makes room for progress; the proud man believes he is already there.   [776

PROMISCUITY

If a man is really made better and saner because he gives way to his sexual instincts and is uninhibited by the Christian law of lifelong marriage, why should not a man be better because he gives way to other instincts, such as the hunting instinct? Why not organize a "kill your enemy" hunt, uninhibited by the moral taboo of a Fifth Commandment?   [777

PROMISE

... **Consolation.**   There can be little consolation for a thousand donkeys dying of starvation to know that the thousandth-and-first donkey is to have fields of clover.   [778

PROPERTY

Power is distributed through history, as property is distributed . . . Property involves responsibility and the surrender of responsibility is the surrender of freedom. Keep our souls free on the inside by obeying God's laws; keep our

souls free on the outside by a wide diffusion of property, and
we will preserve our peace and our prosperity.   [779

PROTEST

... **Rebellion.** Two aspects of contemporary rebellion
may be noticed. The first is that, unlike the old revolution-
ists, the protestors are without a program. They dig holes,
but they put nothing in them. But more important still is the
second aspect: the lack of positive movement toward re-
pentence, holiness, Christ-likeness, to counteract this rebellion . . . What positive action is being taken by the
faithful, the shepherds and the sheep to stop this descent
from Divinity to humanity to bestiality? Because "God is
dead," as the placards say, is the Devil dead also?   [780

... **Revolt.** Revolting against the whole of existence, a
soul thinks that it has disproved it; it begins to admire its
own torment as a protest against life.   [781

PROVIDENCE

... **Views Of.** Treatises on Providence have too closely
followed the Greek and too distantly the Hebrew. The
Greek view conceived of an ideal world realized in time;
everything in the world was the concretion of an archetypal
idea existing in the mind of God. For the Hebrew, the world
is not yet the complete actualization of the transcendent
purposes of God, because the purposes of God are eschato-
logical. The Greek view regarded religion as rational; the
Hebrew as historical . . . it viewed man in relation to the
transcendent purposes of God.   [782

PSYCHIATRY

... **Modern Need.** Psychiatry is not as much a modern discovery as a modern need. Its method has been known for centuries, but there was never occasion to apply it, because in other ages men knew they could not "get away with it." Their purgations, reparations and amendments were settled on their knees in prayer, rather than on their backs on a couch. [783

... **Moralists.** When the moralist gets into the abnormal where psychiatry belongs and denies the necessity of psychiatry, he is out of his field. When the psychiatrist denies freedom, responsibility, guilt and says that we are all sex-determined, he is out of his field. Disease is one thing; guilt another. [784

... **Necessity.** As our civilization breaks down, the science of psychiatry becomes increasingly necessary. Neuroses and psychoses are just as real as cancer and tuberculosis. [785

... **Theology.** In actual fact, no moral theologian denies the validity and necessity of psychiatry; but since many analysts do deny the realms of the moral, the Divine, and the supernatural, it is important to continue stressing the difference between the two. [786

PSYCHOANALYSIS

To the extent that psychoanalysis, in the twentieth century, takes an interest in the inside of a man's soul, it represents a great progress over the sociologies of the nineteenth century, which thought that everything that was wrong in the world was due to poverty, bad economic conditions, free trade, high tariffs, or politics. Furthermore, to the extent that psychoanalysis has revealed the effects of our minds—even of the unconscious mind—on our physical health and behavior, it has confirmed the great Christian truth that an uncontrolled mind (or even an uncontrolled unconsciousness) leads to abnormality. [787

There are thousands of patients on their backs who would be made better if they were on their knees instead. [788

"Psychoanalysis" becomes very wrong indeed when it ceases to be a method of treatment and pretends to be a philosophy. [789

PSYCHOLOGY
When we explain away our conceits by psychological jargon we increase our inner mental discomfort, as the denial of a physical illness gives random speed to the disease. [790

...Materialist. Materialist psychology believes in a passive abandonment of the soul, in which the higher part of the personality gives free rein to the lower part and its spontaneous appetites. It falsely believes that, by living according to animal inheritance, personality will receive back from the mysterious animal forces those gifts of creativity which the sick soul has lost. [791

...Soul Study. To study souls is nothing new; in the whole gamut of modern psychology there is nothing written on frustration, fears, and anxieties which can even faintly compare in depth or breadth with St. Thomas's treatise on the Passions, St. Augustine's *Confessions,* or Bossuet's treatise on Concupiscence. [792

... **Teachings.** Psychologists teach that the needs of the id are more important than the ideals of the super-ego, that a discipline of sex ends in a tension and neurosis which can be released only by carnal abandonment—these men have increased the world's selfishness, egotism, and cruelty. [793

PSYCHOSYNTHESIS

More than any form of psychoanalysis, the world needs psychosynthesis, for human beings need to be put together more than they need to be taken apart. [794

PUBLICITY

... **Glory.** Publicity is the rouge on the anemic cheek or ordinariness; glory is the bloom which is the sign of health. [795

PUNISHMENT

... **Mercy.** When David sinned, God gave him the choice of being punished either by Him or by man. David chose God because His Mercy is greater. [796

... **Sins.** Everyone who is conscious of sin knows that his sin deserves punishment, but if sin or guilt is denied, the need for punishment finds its outlet vicariously in a love of violence visited upon others. [797

PURGATORY

There is one word which to modern ears probably signifies the unreal, the fictional, and even the absurd in the Christian vision of life, and that is the word "purgatory." . . . The necessity of purgatory is grounded upon the absolute purity of God. In the Book of the Apocalypse we read of the great beauty of His city, of the pure gold, with its walls of jasper and its spotless light which is not of the sun nor the moon but the light of the lamb slain from the beginning of the world. We also learn of the condition of entering the gates of that heavenly Jerusalem: "There shall not enter into it anything defiled, or that worketh abomination, or maketh a lie, but they that are written in the book of the life of the Lamb." Justice demands that nothing unclean, but only the pure of heart shall stand before the face of a pure God. If there were no purgatory, then the justice of God would be too terrible for words, for who are they who would dare assert themselves pure enough and spotless enough to stand before the immaculate Lamb of God?   [798

Take away purgatory, and God could not pardon so easily, for will an act of contrition at the edge of the tomb atone for thirty years of sinning? Take away purgatory and the infinite justice of God would have to reject from Heaven those who resolve to pay their debts, but have not yet paid the last farthing . . . for, regardless of how trivial the fault, God cannot pardon without tears, and there are no tears in Heaven.   [799

PURITY

A society that needs healing and regeneration will receive it mostly from the innocent. The pure can look on the impure without contempt. [800

...Definition. What is purity? Purity is reverence for mystery . . . Purity is reverence for the mystery of creation . . . It is this consciousness of mystery which produces chivalry in the teen-ager, though he does not know its meaning, nor could he explain it. [801

...Definition. Purity is not something negative; it is not just an unopened bud; it is not something cold; it is not ignorance of life. Is justice merely the absence of dishonesty? Is mercy merely the absence of cruelty? Is faith merely the absence of doubt? Purity is not merely the absence of sensuality; it is selflessness born of love and the highest love of all. [802

...Will. Purity does not begin in the body, but in the will. From there it flows outwards, cleansing thought, imagination, and, finally, the body. Bodily purity is a repercussion or echo of the will. Life is impure only when the will is impure. [803

PURPOSE

...God's Law. We do not attain the purposes we seek by violating God's laws; but we hurt ourselves . . . The will to power is self defeating. In piercing God's heart, it is our own that we slay. [804

...**Man.** As the eye was made for seeing and the ear for hearing, so the mind was made for truth; as the stomach was made for digestion and the heart was made for pumping the blood, so the will was made for goodness and for love.   [805

...**Progress.** When there is no goal or over-all purpose, people generally concentrate on motion. Instead of working toward an ideal, they keep changing the ideal and calling it "progress."   [806

...**Youth.** Our delinquent youths in America become delinquent because they have no missions, no purpose in life. Pour steam into a boiler and give it no work and it will blow up. Youth is "blowing up" for the same reason.   [807

··R··

RACIAL SUPERIORITY

The false idea of the superiority of certain races and classes is due to the forgetfulness of the spiritual foundations of equality. We of the Western world have been rightly proud of the fact that we have a civilization superior to others. But we have given the wrong reason for that superiority. We assume that we are superior because we are white. We are not. We are superior because we are Christians. The moment we cease to be Christian, we will revert to the barbarism from which we came.   [808

READING

...**Books.** Our minds were not meant to rust in us unused. Books are readily available, and what companions they are! A good book is the same today as yesterday. It is never displeased when we put it down; it is always inspiring when we pick it up. It never fails us in times of adversity.
[809

...**Discrimination.** Taste a book or magazine before reading, it may be bitter or even rotten. The mind is more important than the stomach. Just as some food is fit only for the garbage pail, so some reading is not fit for the mind. A mind that does not perfect itself by good reading does not remain the same, it becomes duller. White fences do not remain white fences; muscles that are not used atrophy, and a mind that does not take mental nourishment can starve.

[810

REASON

... Grace. Man cannot redeem himself by his own reason or his own power; but man can use both reason and power in cooperation with Divine Grace, and this is what he does when he becomes converted. It is time now to talk of the effect such a conversion has on the soul. The soul is now open to the working of Sanctifying Grace, which elevates our nature so that we *become* something we were not naturally—partakers of the Divine Nature Who descended to the level of our mortality to make us share His Life. This new grace, which adds Divine to human filiation so that we become Children of God as well as children of our parents, is not extrinsic to the soul or a mere imputation of the merit of Christ. There is a reality in the soul which was not there before—a created reality which comes directly from God Himself, a reality which we ourselves cannot merit in the strict sense of the term. That is why it is called a grace; it is *gratis,* or free.

[811

... Judgment. To be able to use reason and good judgment when everyone else goes to pieces not only saves self, but also neighbor.

[812

... Judgment. Reason is used to create sham doubts and to weave cloaks with which to cover our real motives. No wonder God must judge us—we are so slow to judge ourselves. [813

... **Knowledge.** We can look at a painting, and guess perhaps the period in which it was painted, and something of the skill and technique of the artist. But we could look on the painting from now until the crack of doom without ever knowing the inmost thoughts of the artist. If we were ever to know those, he would have to tell us. So, too, we can look upon this world with our reason. We can know something of the power of God from the mountains and the sea, something of His beauty from the sunset, something of His purity from the snow, but we could plunge into the depths of the earth and scan the skies without ever knowing the inmost thoughts of God. If we were ever to know them, He would have to reveal them to us. [814

... **Men; Women.** Women use reason best at the point where man loses it. Passion impairs reason in a man; in a woman it does not. [815

REBELLION
... **Children.** Perhaps if we inquire into the rebellion of children against their parents, we may find that they have some instinctive feeling that the parents have no right to command them, but they cannot put their finger on it. Could it not be this: Where do their parents get the authority to command them? Do they recognize that authority? [816

RECLAMATION
Centuries ago, according to a story perhaps apocryphal, in the streets of Florence there stood a beautiful piece of

Carrara marble that had been cut and hacked and ruined by some cheap artist. Other mediocre artists passed it by, and bemoaned that it should have been so ruined. One day Michelangelo passed it and asked that it be brought to his studio. He there applied to it his chisel, his genius, and his inspiration. He drew out of it the immortal statue of David. The lesson contained herein is that there is nothing so base or low that it cannot be reconquered, that there is no duty however menial that cannot be retrieved for sanctity, and that there is nothing that is cast down that cannot be lifted up. [817

REDEMPTION

Virtue is possible only in those spheres in which it is possible to be vicious; sacrifice is possible only on those levels on which it is possible to be selfish; redemption is possible only in those realms where it is possible to be enslaved. [818

Down in the gutter of a city street was a drop of water, soiled, dirty, and stagnant. Way up in the heavens a gentle sunbeam saw it, leaped out its azure sky, down to the drop, kissed it, thrilled it through and through with new strange life and hope, and lifted it up higher and higher and higher, beyond the clouds, and one day let it fall as a flake of immaculate snow on a mountaintop. [819

... Self-Sacrifice. Pain, suffering, error, lies, false charges, all fit into the redemptive pattern, for the victory of Christ is not merely *over* death but *through* death, for it is the victory of self-sacrifice, and self-sacrifice is never complete until life is given. [820

. . . Strength. Sometimes the part of the house that is repaired is the strongest part in the end. [821

REFORMERS

. . . Moral. All human appeals, arguments, and coaxings toward moral betterment—like all psychological appeals to a morally disordered soul—are external to the person to be reformed. Since the action comes from without, the reformer can only ring the bell—he cannot get inside of the house, and he has no ally within its doors. [822

RELIGION

. . . Cosmic. Not many men want to die to their lower selves; it costs so much. Some prefer to have a cosmic religion, which puts no restraint on their pride, nor curbs their passions. [823

. . . Divine. Religion does not seem pleasant to those who have never climbed high enough, by a renunciation of selfishness, to glimpse its vistas; but a divine religion with the Holy Eucharist is much more pleasant to those who experience it than the world is pleasant to those who sin in it. It is possible that a true lover of God may have tasted both worlds, both lives, if he is a convert or a penitent. But the man who has lived only for the flesh, pleasure, and profit has no experience whatever of the thrills of the spirit. Since he has never tasted, he never can compare. [824

. . . Hatred. The man who hates religion does so because of the evil in his life. [825

... Hatred Of. The final form of hatred of religion is a wish to defy God and to maintain one's own evil in the face of His goodness and power. [826

... Individual. An individual religion can be as misleading and uninformed as an individual astronomy or an individual mathematics. [827

... Persecutors. Since those who persecute religion as a form of escapism must constantly think about God and His Church, it follows that they are often closer to conversion than the indifferent man of a Western Liberal Civilization, who does not trouble making up his mind on any ultimate question. [828

... Personal. We did not wait until we were twenty-one and then, after studying the Constitution, decide to become Americans. We were born American—born out of the womb of America. So likewise, in the spiritual order, we are born out of the womb of the Church. Never therefore say: Religion is a personal matter. You can no more have your personal religion than you can have your personal sun. If your personal religion unites you to God, and my personal religion unites me to God, then is there not a common relationship between us to a common Father? [829

... Politics. Never before in history has the spiritual been so unprotected against the political; never before has the political so usurped the spiritual. It is not religion that is meddling in politics; it is politics that is meddling in religion. [830

...Popularity. The fact is religion is popular only when it ceases to be truly religious. Religion by its very nature is unpopular—certainly unpopular with the ego.   [831

...Sacrifice. Religion requires sacrifice; it is not a crutch, but a cross. It is not an escape, it is a burden; not a flight, but a response. One leans on a crutch, but a cross rests on us. A coward can use a crutch, but it takes a hero to embrace a cross.   [832

...Weakened. Almost everyone today wants religion, but everyone wants a religion that does not cost too much; that is why Christianity has been watered down to suit the modern mind.   [833

RELIGIOUS PERSECUTION

Persecution of religion is a sign of the indefensibility of the antireligious or atheistic attitude, for by the violence of hate it hopes to escape the irrationality of Godlessness. [834

REMORSE

...Effects Of. When remorse scourges, the old ego becomes mad and even more violent than ever before. Temper flares, hatred of others multiplies as a projection of a disguised hatred of self, and a despondency seizes the soul from which no distraction gives relief. But all these violent outbursts against virtue are really nothing but the gathering of dark and angry clouds which one day will be dissolved in showers.   [835

...Sorrow. Unless we are ready to ask for the forgiveness of our sins by God, the examination of conscience may be only a vain form of introspection, which can make a soul worse if it ends in *remorse* instead of *sorrow*. For the two are quite distinct: Judas had remorse. Peter had sorrow. Judas "repented unto himself," as Scripture tells us; Peter, unto the Lord. As a psychic malady sometimes results from a failure to adjust self to the right environment, so a moral evil results from the failure of the soul to adjust itself to God. Despair is such a failure—Judas despaired, but Peter hoped. Despair comes from unrelatedness, from the refusal of a soul to turn to God.   [836

REPRESSION

If there were ever any nonsense in the world, it is the notion that repression is always wrong. It assumes that nothing should ever be repressed. This is to forget that if you repress evil, good comes up; if you repress good, evil comes up; if you repress the idea that you are going to rob a bank, honesty asserts itself; if a soldier represses the temptation that he ought to sleep while he is on guard, duty asserts itself. The problem is not whether there will be repression or not; it is rather what will be repressed—goodness or evil!
                                                                      [837

... **Christian.** Christianity, like modern paganism, believes that repression is harmful, but it makes a necessary distinction. Christianity says that the repression of evil thoughts, desires, and acts—such as the urge to kill, despoil, calumniate, rob, injure, covet, hate—is good for the soul; it deplores the repression of guilt or sin through a denial of the need of confession. And it states that the repression of actual

graces, inspirations to a good life, and the urge to sacrifice
self for neighbor is bad for the soul. [838

... **Zeal.** Our Lord did not repress the intense emotional
zeal of Paul; He merely redirected it from hate to love. Our
Lord did not repress the biological vitalities of a Magdalene;
He merely turned her passion from love of vice to love of virtue. Such a conversion of energies explains why the greatest
sinners—like Augustine—sometimes make the greatest
saints; it is not because they have been sinners that they love
God with their special intensity, but because they have
strong urges, violent passions, flowing emotions which,
turned to holy purposes, now do as much good as they once
did harm . . . there may be a greater potentiality for the
Christian apostolate in revolutionary Russia than is apparent
in the indifference and false tolerance of the neither hot nor
cold liberals of Western Civilization. God can do more with
fire than He can with tepid water. [839

REPUTATION

The greatness of any age is to be measured by those whom
it holds in high repute. [840

The most lasting reputations are those that are achieved
after death when the tinsel of empty glory fades away. The
greatness of Lincoln is posthumous. The glory of Christ
came after His Crucifixion. And from Him has come this
warning: "Woe to you when all men speak well of
you." [841

RESPECTABILITY

Typical of respectability was Lord Chesterfield in his *Letters to His Son*, which constituted, for generations, the text-

book of civility and politeness. The letters of Lord Chesterfield were written to his son Philip when he was only eight years of age. Philip, however, developed into a clumsy, untidy young man of slovenly habits. He stammered all his life and was a great disappointment to Lord Chesterfield. The keynote of respectability is in the line of Chesterfield: "He ought to know about religion and morals and to preserve the appearance of both." It was for this reason that Doctor Johnson said of the letters of Chesterfield "that they taught little more than the morals of a 'rotter' and the manners of a dancing master." [842

RESPONSIBILITY
... Liberty. It must be remembered that every flight from responsibility is a flight from liberty . . . Perhaps it is the very burden of responsibility that flows from free choice that makes so many ready to surrender their great gift of freedom. [843

REVELATION
... Reason. Revelation does not demand a complete break with reason, either on the part of the subject who receives the revelation, or on the part of God Who gives it. It follows that when God prepares the climax of His Providence, He will bring into it all the common characteristic lines along which human thought has groped for the Divine. [844

REVOLT
... Modern World. The revolt of the modern child against his parents is a miniature of the revolt of the modern world against the memory of 1900 years of Christian culture

and the great Hebrew, Grecian, and Roman cultures which preceded them. Any respect for that tradition is called "reactionary," with the result that the modern soul has developed a commentator mentality which judges yesterday by today, and today by tomorrow.   [845

REVOLUTION

Revolution is a creature of the past, not of the future . . . The protests of a revolution may be right, but no revolution ever completely realizes its promised reforms.   [846

. . . **Communism.** Communists are right in saying this world needs a revolution, but not their cheap kind, which merely transfers booty and loot out of one man's pocket into another's. We need the kind of revolution that will purge out of a man's heart pride and covetousness and lust and anger.   [847

RIDICULE

Ridicule covers up the disgust of one's own life by projecting that disgust to others. Evil people ridicule the good. Since goodness is a reproach to them, they become very destructive of it.   [848

RIGHT

. . . **Wrong.** There is no sense in saying anything is wrong, unless we know what is right.   [849

. . . **Wrong.** If one accepts the false philosophy of life that there is no absolute distinction between right and wrong, that good and evil depend solely upon one's point of view, that the individual himself is determinant of virtue and vice, and then adds to it some very evil deeds in keeping with that philosophy, it will not be long until conscience is drugged and even killed. [850

RIGHTS

...God-Given. Man has rights and liberties previous to any constitution, and because they are God-derived, and not man-derived, it follows that no State can ever take them away. That is why our government recognizes that the rights of man are broader than the Constitution as is stated in Amendment 9 of the Constitution: "The enumeration in the Constitution of certain rights, shall not be construed to deny or disparage others retained by the people." [851

RISK

Those who would pluck flowers from the edge of the precipice must be prepared to fall. [852

ROMANCE

...Life. The assumption is that life is a perpetual honeymoon, and that the present moment is eternal. The thrill of holding hands, or of watching waves roll on a moonlit beach, will never end. This false romantic idea is fostered in part by movies, where a plot is worked up to an arbitrary climax in which the boy and girl are married. This is assumed to be the end, when actually it is only the beginning. [853

RUSSIA

In a not too distant day Russia, like the prodigal son, will return to the father's house. Let not Western civilization refuse to accept it back or absent itself from the feast celebrating the salvation of what was lost. [854

... **Communism.** We must make a distinction between Russia and Communism. Russia is a people; Communism is an ideology. The people endure with their tradition and culture; ideologies pass. Nazism is dead but the German people live on. [855

... **Communism.** The foreign policy of Russia is a tactic; it is by the philosophy of Communism that Russia is to be judged. [856

... **End of Communism.** I think we will live to see the end of communism in Russia. Communism has no way of propagating its masters. The monarchy has; democracy has; communism has none, except exile, cutting throats. Good is self-preserving; evil is always self-defeating. [857

... **Religion; The Soviet Constitution** ... Article 124 reads, "Freedom of religious worship and freedom of antireligious propaganda are recognized for all of the citizens." "Freedom of worship" is recognized if you can find a church. The Communists closed 52,000 of them and liquidated the clergy. May you preach religion? May you broadcast religion? May you publish tracts on religion? *No.* That is *propaganda,* and the Constitution states that the right of antireligious propaganda belongs to the Soviets, but the right to propagate the Faith does not exist in Communist Russia. [858

...Zeal. When Russia receives the gift of faith, its role will be that of an apostle to the rest of the world. It will help bring faith to the rest of the world. Why are we so hopeful about Russia? Why should it be the means of evangelizing nations of the earth? Because Russia has fire; Russia has zeal. God could do something with the hate of a Saul, by turning it into love. He could do something with the passion of a Magdalene, by converting it to zeal; but God can do nothing with those who are neither hot nor cold. These He will vomit from His Mouth. [859

· · S · ·

SACRIFICE

... **Love.** A young man loves a young woman and gives
her a ring of gold instead of tin. The day that men forget
that love is synonymous with sacrifice, they will ask what
kind of cruel and ruthless creature was that woman who
asked for a ring of gold instead of tin. The day that man
forgets that love is synonymous with sacrifice, he will ask
what kind of a God is it who asks for mortification and
self-denial.   [860

... **Rearing Children.** The rearing of children demands
sacrifice, without which, like unwatered flowers, they wilt
and die.   [861

SAINTS

As the rays of the sun are so rich that we cannot see their
many splendors unless they are shot through a prism, which
causes them to break into the seven rays of the spectrum, so,
too, the Life of Christ which the saints reflect, is so infinitely
Good, that it takes an infinite variety of saints shot through
the prism of love and penance to reflect the holiness of the

Son of God. Sinners are always alike; saints are always different. [862

... **Values.** A saint does not put forth any more energy, in being a saint, than the head of an advertising agency does to get business, or an athlete does in training for a fight, or a college boy does to get into a fraternity, or a woman does to get into a size ten dress each Spring. The difference lies in their sense of values. The simple truth is that it does not require much time to make a saint; it only requires much love. The difference, however, is that we are escapists and the saints are not. The saints go all the way, but we hold back. [863

SALVATION

We are willing to be saved from poverty, from war, from ignorance, from disease, from economic insecurity; such types of salvation leave our individual whims and passions and concupiscences untouched. That is one of the reasons why social Christianity is so very popular, why there are many who contend that the business of Christianity is to do nothing but to help in slum clearance or the development of international amity. [864

... **Saving Others.** People cannot be made clean by scolding them or by lecturing them or by patronizing them. We have to go down to the filth if we mean to lift them out. Nothing can be repulsive, if it means the saving of your brother. [865

... **The World.** The Church says the purpose of man in saving himself is also that of saving the world. [866

SCANDAL

The fondness of the twentieth century for scandal is due to a great extent to its guilty conscience. [867

SCAPEGOATS

Many of the troubles of today come about because everyone is looking for someone else whom he can blame for his wrongdoing. Some of the favorite scapegoats are a mother who has loved the sinner too much or a father who did not love enough. For the Nazis, the scapegoat was the Jews; for the Communists, it is the Christians; for the Freudians, it is sometimes called a repression due to "totems and taboos." [868

SCIENCE

Science is not atheistic and godless. Physical science is not concerned with God, or religion, or moral values. It is just as wrong to accuse empirical science of being atheistic as to accuse a speaker of being anti-American because in his speech he does not quote the Constitution of the United States. [869

Science has done everything it could to make us feel at home on earth. Suddenly it produces something which could make us all homeless. [870

... God And Science. If the laws of psychology are not applicable to astronomy, and the laws of music not transferable to law, and the predicates of an amoeba not applicable to a Pantheon, why should the categories of physics, psychology and sociology be applicable to God? [871

... Judgment. If philosophy can no longer judge science, then science is its own justification; it can be used as well for purposes of destruction as for human betterment, and no one can pass judgment on its morality.   [872

... Modern Man. The modern man, finding that Humanism and Sex both fail to satisfy, seeks his happiness in Science . . . But Science fails too, for it is something more than a knowledge of matter the soul craves.   [873

... Philosophy; Ethics. Science cannot give us a philosophy, because it immerses man in nature and avoids the important subject of his destiny. It cannot give us an ethics because science by itself is unmoral. Morality comes from its ends, and science is indifferent to ends.   [874

... Religion And Science. How could science be any enemy of religion when God commanded man to be a scientist the day He told him to rule the earth and subject it?   [875

... Scientists. Sometimes a mathematical law supplants God, as it did in the case of Babylon when, with the discovery of the stellar cosmos, certain Chaldean mathematicians transferred their allegiance from Marduk-Bel to seven planets. The same mentality is seen in the Western man of science.   [876

SECURITY

... Temporal. An overemphasis on temporal security is a compensation for a loss of the sense of eternal security.
          [877

SELF-CONQUEST

Each new conquest of self is a new thrill, for each repeated act brings closer and closer that love we fall just short of in all love, eternal union with Our Lord and Savior.
[878

SELF-DENIAL

The tens of thousands who in the past year have tried to give up smoking cigarettes, and then, after twenty-four hours, saw their resolution go up in smoke, can testify how little the modern mind is prepared for any kind of real sacrifice or self-denial.
[879

... **Mortification.** Self-denial is no pale shrinking from the light, no object creeping on earth, no self-inflicted pain. In the East, pain is for the sake of pain; it is an end in itself. In Christianity, mortification is a means to an end, and the end is charity. Hence St. Paul said that if he should deliver up his body to be burned and have not Divine love, then it profiteth him nothing.
[880

SELF-DISCIPLINE

Self-discipline is not an end in itself but a means to an end. Those who make self-discipline the essence of religion reject some of God's creatures as evil. Generally they become proud. But detachment, properly practiced, is only a means of attachment to God. When there is no love of Him, there is no true self-descipline. St. Paul tells us the philanthropy, sacrifice, alms, even martyrdom, if embraced for any reason except love of God does not deserve an eternal reward. [881

...Flesh; Spirit. Anyone who makes the taming of animal impulses the end and prime purpose of his life—as some of the Oriental mystics do—achieves the negation of the flesh but not the affirmation of the spirit. [882

...Not Understood. The disciplining of the self-will, the taming of the ego, the pruning of selfishness, the sacrificing of our wishes, are today little understood by those who regard self-negation as frustration, and self-expression as an ideal. [883

SELF-DISCOVERY

The discovery that we are to blame for being the way we are is greater than the discovery made by any explorer. Such a discovery of our own fault is impossible unless there be a higher standard outside ourselves, from whose love we know that we have fallen. [884

SELF-EXPRESSION

If abandonment to the passions and animal lust is the pathway to self-expression, then what consolation shall an individual seek in old age? Such a philosophy may satisfy young animals, but not old animals. [885

Our generation has been raised on the idea of 'self-expression' which, being translated negatively, means there should never be any self-restraint. Every desire and impulse which satisfies the ego is considered good; any form of self-denial, or repression of biological urges, is considered as harmful to the personality. The ego is flattered and pampered, even to a point where children are raised on the theory that they should never be disciplined, much less punished or reprimanded for their selfishness.   [886

SELF-INTEREST

Men emerge interested in the question of whether they are at the top of the class, or the foot, or somewhere in the middle, working their way higher. This interest in the self and its rating poisons the proud man's life—for self-centeredness is always a form of pride.   [887

When we are preoccupied with ourselves we do not give our full attention to any person or thing that comes our way, and so we do not get, from each experience, the enjoyment it could give to us. It is because the small child knows that he is small, and accepts the fact without pretending to be big, that his world is a world of wonders. To every little boy, his father is a giant.   [888

SELFISHNESS

... **Marriage.** A young man who is egotistical and selfish before marriage will have that selfishness increased in geometrical proportion after marriage. For every ten dozen of flowers she gets before the engagement, she will only get one dozen afterward, but for every bottle of Four Roses he drinks before marriage, there will be four bottles of Four Roses after.   [889

... **Sin.** Selfishness is the world's greatest sin; that is why the world hates those who hate it, why it is jealous of those who have more; why it is envious of those who do more; why it dislikes those who refuse to flatter, and why it scorns those who tell us the truth about ourselves; its whole life is inspired by the egotistical, and the personal, and its wrath is born of that self-love. [890

SELF-JUDGMENT

We justify want of faith by saying, "I don't go to Church, but I am better than those who do," as one might say, "I don't pay taxes or serve the nation, but I am better than those who do." If each man is his own judge and standard, then who shall say he is wrong? [891

SELF-KNOWLEDGE

... Analysis. The basic difference between psychological analysis and self-knowledge is that, in the former, we are spectators, as we might be in the theater. But under conscience we are our own creators; we see ourselves as making or breaking our character. [892

SELF-LOVE

... Self-Hate. A person often tries to "get away from himself," through alcohol, dissipation, and drugs. The self one has to live with can be one's own greatest punishment. To be left forever with that self which we hate is hell. He who starts only loving self ends by hating himself; he becomes like a mansion lying forlorn, spacious, and empty. [893

SELF-REFLECTION

Self-reflection is necessary because we are all very much like onions. We are surrounded by coats and coats and coats of hypocrisy and deceit, masks and artifices. At the center of these is the core of character. We cry when we peel onions; we also cry when we strip ourselves of the coats of hypocrisy and see ourselves as we really are.   [894

SELF-RIGHTEOUSNESS

... **Heaven.** Christ said that the harlots and the Quislings would enter the Kingdom of Heaven before the self-righteous and the smug.   [895

... **"Nice People".** The nice people rarely come to God; they take their moral tone from the society in which they live. Like the Pharisee in the front of the temple, they believe themselves to be very respectable citizens. Elegance is their test of virtue; to them the moral is the aesthetic, the evil is the ugly. Every move they make is dictated, not by a love of goodness, but by the influence of their age. Their intellects are cultivated through knowledge of current events; they read only the best sellers; but their hearts are undisciplined. They say that they would go to Church if the Church were only better—but they never tell you how much better the Church must be before they will join it.
[896

SEX

The person is in search of the absolute, i.e., perfect happiness. To use sex as a substitute for the absolute is a vain attempt to turn the copy into the original.   [897

... **Adjustment.** Rhinoceroses are sexually adjusted, but they do not love.   [898

226

... **Creativeness.** The mystery of creativeness is surrounded with awe. A special reverence does envelop the power to be co-creators with God in the making of human life. It is this hidden element which in a special way belongs to God, as does the grace of God in the sacraments. Those who speak of sex alone concentrate on the physical or visible element, forgetting the spiritual or invisible mystery of creativeness. [899

... **Deification.** The principal reason for sex deification is loss of belief in God. Once men lose God, they lose the purpose of life; and when the purpose of living is forgotten, the universe becomes meaningless. Man then tries to forget his emptiness in the intensity of a momentary experience. [900

... **Love.** Sex is biological and physiological and has its definite zones of satisfaction. Love, on the contrary, includes all of these but is directed to the totality of the person loved, i.e., as a creature composed of body and soul and made to the image and likeness of God. [901

... **Love.** When sex is divorced from love there is a feeling that one has been stopped at the vestibule of the castle of pleasure; that the heart has been denied the city after crossing the bridge. Sadness and melancholy result from such a frustration of destiny, for it is the nature of man to be sad when he is pulled outside himself, or exteriorized without getting any nearer his goal. There is a closer correlation between mental instability and the animal view of sex than many suspect. [902

... Love. Those who identify love with sex vainly believe that they can give the totality of themselves to those whom they love. This is impossible, because man has a soul as well as a body. In all love, the body can be given, but not the soul; in all love the body can be received but not the soul. That is why in that kind of love, the desire to lose self always fails, but after love's action, one is thrown back upon self feeling even more lonely than before. The sense of emptiness and of isolation is due to the fact that one seeks the infinite in the other. The infinite alone is in God. In vain does one seek the soul in the flesh alone. Such persons who have reduced love to a biological function always feel at the end of it that it was someone else they loved; the one they claimed to love having escaped them.   [903

... Lovers. The greatest illusion of lovers is to believe that the intensity of their sexual attraction is the guarantee of the perpetuity of their love. It is because of this failure to distinguish between the glandular and spiritual—or between sex which we have in common with animals, and love which we have in common with God—that marriages are so full of deception.   [904

... Man. It was not true, as Freud said, that man must be understood in terms of sex; rather it is sex that must be understood in terms of man. As the planets revolve around the sun, so must the function of the body revolve about the personality. When the planets leave their orbit, they burn out in space; when sex is separated from human personality, it burns out as two epidermic contacts.   [905

... Marital Love. In married love there is something

personal, something social. The personal is the deliberate will to love the other; the social is that side of the body-unity which is automatic and of a reflex nature and which to some extent is outside personal control. It is this reflex character of body-love which indicates that God has a hand in every personal love, for by it He preserves the human race.   [906

... **Overemphasis.** A reason for the overemphasis on sex is the modern denial of immortality. Once the Eternal is denied, the Now becomes all-important.   [907

... **Problems.** The modern Epicureans are those who believe that passion is what is best and highest in man, and should always be satisfied . . . This group believes that one of the reasons the past generation had social problems is that the passion of sex was so hushed up. They argue that if it were brought into the open, all problems resulting from sex would cease. As a matter of fact we have given the problem of sex in our generation as much ventilation as Swiss cheese has holes, but we have not done away with divorce, juvenile delinquency, or sex problems.   [908

... **Soul.** Sex in isolation from personality does not exist! An arm living and gesticulating apart from the living organism is an impossibility. Man has no organic functions isolated from his soul. There is involvement of the whole personality. Nothing is more psychosomatic than the union of two in one flesh; nothing so much alters a mind, a will, for better or for worse. The separation of soul and body is death. Those who separate sex and spirit are rehearsing for death.   [909

SHAME

Shame draws a veil over the deepest instincts, holding them in check until they can satisfy both body and soul. It guards the person against a too precocious revelation of its instincts, and bears witness to the fact that there is some great mystery and sanctity attached to the body such as Paul referred to when he said, "The body is for the Lord." [910

SICKNESS

Sickness prevents many a man from being a scoundrel and gives him a chance to mend his ways. [911

SILENCE

The silence of the Lord clamored more in Herod's ear than did the loud rebuke of John the Baptist. Such silence is thunder, for it is the penalty that God inflicts on the soul that is not sincere. [912

... **Communion.** Silence is not a privation of stillness, not a muteness, not an emptiness; it is a communion by which one attains truths above creation and action. [913

... **Privacy.** There is almost a conspiracy against silence and privacy. [914

... **Speech.** Silence of the right kind is as deep as eternity, whereas speech is as shallow as time. [915

SIN

Nobody likes to hear the word "sin" today, but we will begin to be happier when we realize that maybe most of our trouble comes from the fact that we are sinners . . . Those who say that sin begets "a guilt complex" hope to scare the cure away by name calling. Because a person is sick and asks for a physician, does he have "a sickness complex?"   [916

... **Denial.** Sin is most serious, and the tragedy is deepened by the denial that we are sinners. If the blind deny that they are blind, how shall they ever see? The really unforgivable sin is the denial of sin, because, by its nature, there is now nothing to be forgiven.   [917

... **Essence Of.** The essence of sin is not a negation of a code but a rejection of a person toward whom one feels bound through his goodness and his love.   [918

... **Nature Of.** There is no cement in sin; its nature is centrifugal, divisive and disruptive.   [919

... **Virtues.** Sins do not become virtues by being widely practiced. Right is still right if nobody is right, and wrong is wrong if everybody is wrong. Some have contended that sex aberrations are as common as the common cold, but nobody has so far asked us to consider the cold normal and desirable.   [920

... **Weakness.** Often the sins we most loudly condemn in others are those to which we are most secretly attached, or else constitute our greatest weakness.   [921

SINCERITY

A farmer may be sincere in planting thistles, but he will not raise corn.   [922

SINNERS

... Christ's Interest.   He was interested in sinners not because of their merits, but because of their misery.   [923

... Realization.   To be a sinner is our distress, but to know it is our hope.   [924

SINS

... Good And Evil.   The good want their sins forgiven; the evil want them explained away. The good recover peace of soul; the evil have to be satisfied with peace of mind. The explanation of this phenomenon is that the good have another principle of action in them than the evil. The evil are guided solely by the thought either of the satisfaction of the flesh or the spirit and that this world is all. But the good have another principle in them, entirely above nature which is called grace and by which they are united to God.   [925

SLAVERY

Marx and Freud were right in dealing with slavery as one of man's recurring problems, but neither of them understood its nature. Both of them took the inner slavery for granted; both rightly assumed that egotism is normal, one of them studying it in the collective field, the other in the individual. Such egotism is Fallen Man's flaw, recognized by everyone who assumes a Transcendent Source from which man comes and toward which he tends. Some day, some historian with profound insight will show us how external slavery is always the mass production of internal slavery—how man, in slavery to his own lower nature, has attempted to make his condition normal by enslaving others.   [926

SOCIAL REFORM

The reform of outward conduct and enviroment is essential, and it is to this that much civil law is ordained. But it really only deals with the effects and not with the causes; social reformation is only superficial; it is like cutting off the tops of the weeds while the roots are left in the ground. [927

... **Conscience.** It is possible that some persons are prompted to courageous reforms of social injustices by the very inquietude and uneasiness of their individual consciences: knowing that something is wrong on the inside, they attempt to compensate for it by righting the wrong on the outside. This is also the mechanism of those men, who having accumulated great fortunes, try to ease their consciences by subsidizing revolutionary movements.   [928

SOCIAL RESPONSIBILITY

It is not true to say: "The way I conduct my own life is nobody's business but mine," or "it harms nobody else." Could you throw a stone in the sea without causing ripples which would affect even the most distant shore? How then do we think our moral actions can be devoid of social repercussions?   [929

SOCIETY

... **Involvement.** As long as the people are not aroused to abuses or evil, they will not support social legislation. It must be remembered that all crimes against society are founded on false and wicked ideas, and until these are altered, society will not be altered.   [930

... Law of Conscience. Society is merely an interpreter of the law of conscience and not its author. [931

... Reconstruction. Before an architect prepares the plan for a building, he asks who is going to live in it. If criminals are to live in it, he will design a penitentiary; if dogs are to live in it, he will design a doghouse. Before reconstructing society, we must ask the nature of man, who is to live in it. [932

SOLDIERS

The life of the soldier, whether he means it to be or not, is a vicarious one; it is lived for the sake of others. His life is characterized by a surrender of self for others; he does not live for himself; he does not even die for himself. He is fighting the battle of another and for another. He must even run the risk of not enjoying that which he helps to purchase. As Rudyard Kipling put it, "For it's Tommy this, and Tommy that, an' 'Chuck 'im out the brute!' But it's 'Savior of his country' when the guns begin to shoot." [933

... Bible. The greatest tribute that can be paid to soldiers is to recall that they are always well spoken of in the Scripture. Great soldiers are praised—such as Joshua, David and Gideon in the Old Testament. In the New Testament, whenever an individual soldier is mentioned he is the object of veneration and respect. Four Roman soldiers who are mentioned in the New Testament are men of great integrity. [934

... Honor. In a decaying civilization, the last remnants of decency, honor, respect for authority, law and discipline are to be found in the army. Great organizations, like the Roman Empire, begin to die at the center. When the pestilence of moral corruption had infected the governors and the emperors and the counselors of Rome, there were still to be found in the army men of fearless truth, and of incorruptible purity. [935

SORROW

... **Remorse.** Remorse results in worry, jealousy, envy, indignation; but sorrow related to God results in expiation and hope. [936

... **Unity.** People become more united in sorrow than in pleasure. [937

SOUL

... **Atmosphere.** The earth carries its own atmosphere with it as it revolves about the sun; so the soul can carry the atmosphere of God with it, in disregard of turbulent events in the world outside. [938

... **Death.** As St. John tells us in the Apocalypse, "You call yourselves living, and yet you are dead." Just as the life of the body is the soul, so the life of the soul is the grace of God; when the soul leaves the body, the body is dead, and when grace leaves a soul, that soul is dead. [939

... **Inner Conflict.** A soul with a fight inside itself will soon have a fight outside itself with others. [940

SPEECH

... **Freedom Of.** There is a limit to freedom of speech. It is reached when we use freedom of speech to destroy freedom of speech. Anyone may use freedom of speech, as long as he allows anyone else to enjoy that freedom of speech. But there are those who would use this freedom of speech to deny that right to others. Toward that latter group we ought to be intolerant. [941

... **Speaking.** A politician should be able to talk without notes 15 hours on government and national affairs. If he is unable to do so, it would indicate a lack of background for the job. [942

SPIRITUAL LIFE

There are no plains in the spiritual life; we are either going uphill or coming down. [943

The superiority for which men strive today is generally economic or social, not spiritual or moral. When one hears of those who leave the mass-level and dedicate themselves to spiritual perfection, the tendency is to argue: (1) There is nothing in it but an 'escape.' (2) Those who pretend to see something in it are posing. (3) I hate them for it. The reason there is a hatred is because these people in the end may be having something that I do not have. [944

... **Development.** The development of the spiritual, or inner, life is not easy. There is no such thing as the achievement of sanctity in the sense that one finally possesses it as an heirloom, where it remains fixed and stable. Much effort is always required. There is no such thing, for example, as making one's way through some brambles and thorns, overcoming temptations, and finally getting into the clearing of green pastures. The plains are small, and the valleys are narrow; the brief rest given is merely preparation for more brambles and thorns, forests, and even wild beasts, as the struggle must go on even to the end.   [945

SPIRITUAL PROFIT

The greatest spiritual profit comes from loving those who hate us, and from giving gifts and dinners to those who cannot give anything in return, for then recompense will be made in the Kingdom of Heaven.   [946

STUDENTS

...College. College students are beginning to see a tremendous disparity between wisdom and power, that is to say, between the means that we have to exercise power and our knowledge of the final purposes of power. In a certain sense we are like dinosaurs, with great and tremendous bodies, but with tiny little brains that are not capable of choosing what to do with our bodies.   [947

SUBJECTIVISM

If a person grew up under the impression that nobody really cared for him, that he was badly equipped to meet the problems of reality, he, too, would become unusually concerned with himself; his subjectivism, accordingly, would be more of an effect than of a cause of his mental abnormality. The question of subjectivism as an attitude for which the person may be held responsible turns up only after he has become aware of the lack of a foundation for his general approach to reality. It is one aim of mental treatment or

re-education that the neurotic be made to realize the ficti-
tiousness of many things he dreads and, therefore, to see that
his excessive preoccupation with himself is as unnecessary as
it is misguided. [948

SUFFERING

All suffering endured with love of God profits our families
and even the world. [949

... **Love.** Suffering love alone can bring us to our senses
and the real meaning of life. A certain juvenile delinquent
immunized himself from every good influence and sought
every occasion to manifest antisocial behavior. No teaching
or pleading could touch his calloused heart. But he had one
pet, a dog. One day, as he was teaching the dog to do a trick,
he became angry because the dog did not obey him. Like all
who take out their own sins on others, the boy, with a
steel-shod shoe, kicked the dog in the mouth and made it
bleed. When the boy ordered the dog to try the trick again,
the dog first put his jaw up to the boy, then with blood-
stained tongue tried to lick the master's hand; the boy broke
down. Something that beatings, coaxings, restrictions could
not do, suffering love did; it broke him. The Cross with its
unmasked love of pain can unmask the impure pain caused
by our rebellious wills. [950

SUICIDE

Suicidism has become a mental epidemic and a plague
. . . What makes our age sad is not that our joys have
ceased, but our hopes have ceased. [951

SUPERIORITY

...**False.** The false superiority some give themselves is a kind of anesthesia to deaden the pain of being plain fools.

[952

SUPERNATURAL ORDER

The possibility of a supernatural order is not absurd, particularly on the modern premise of the progressive character of the universe.   [953

SURRENDER

...**Peace.** As the whole order of the universe rests on the surrender of the chemicals to the plants, of the plants to the animals, of the animals to man, so that peace of man comes only in the surrender of self to God.   [954

·· T ··

TALENTS

... **Unused.** The talents that are unused are taken away, and the Scriptures tell us that, "But because thou art luke-warm, and neither cold nor hot, I will begin to vomit thee out of my mouth" (Apocalypse 3:16).   [955

TEACHERS

... **Teaching.** The teacher must live intellectually while he is teaching; otherwise, the pupil will not live intellectually either. A professor who is not learning while he is teaching is not a real teacher.   [956

TEACHING

... **Truth; Humility.** Only the mind which humbles itself before the truth it wishes to impart can pass the knowledge on to other minds. The world has never known a humbler teacher than the Word of God Himself, who taught in simple parables and homely examples drawn from sheep and goats and lilies of the field, from patches on worn clothing and wine in new bottles.   [957

TEENAGERS

... **Children.** The difference between a child and a teenager is that a child wants to be loved, a teenager wants to love. [958

... **Creative.** If the teenager is keen on developing his own character, being himself and not someone else, then he creates; he assumes responsibility . . . There are not many, however, who are creative, even among adults. The creative group in society is always the minority . . . Release from inferiority most often comes through imitation. Imitation is an escape from responsibility, the ignoring of character building, a flight from true self-expression, and the avoidance of originality. Imitation enables the ego to assert without being committed to moral values or self-restraint. The teenager then becomes very sensitive to outside influences and is afraid of ever doing anything which is not "the thing." A teenager in such a case never really becomes *himself* or *herself*, but *like* others. [959

... **Love.** Teenagers who fall in love too quickly become enmeshed in the emotional pleasure the other person gives, without ever having time to judge those other qualities of mind and heart which may fall very short of the ideal. One paints with the brush of the infinite the one that is idealized, but then discovers that time wears off the paint. [960

... **Training.** The problem then is not what to do with teenagers; it is who will train them in the Ten Commandments and morality before they are sixteen and seventeen. [961

241

TELEVISION

Our era has been misnamed the "atomic age;" it is rather the "television age." Television influences human brains a thousand times more than the fission and the fusion of atoms. Television is the newborn babe of the Fourth Dimension of Space-Time. Newton knocked the boundaries out of space; Einstein knocked the boundaries out of time, but television has annihilated space and time.   [962

... Dramas. Looking at television dramas . . . is one of the reasons why there is so much torpidity, false tolerance in the face of public crime, tyranny, juvenile delinquency, and corruption of society. The capacity for moral indignation has been lost. People become angry only when their ego has been hurt, but not when truth is outraged.   [963

TEMPTATION

You are not tempted because you are evil; you are tempted because you are *human*.   [964

TENSION

Since it is not you, or I, or he, or she alone that has tension, it must be that the conflict has not a personal origin but is due to human nature itself. The source of the disorder is to be found both in the individual and in humanity itself. A psychology which assumed that all conflicts are due to aberrations in the person himself would fail to account for the universality of conflict. Since everybody is that way, no individual or personal explanation can be the total cause. The personal cause is an effect of the natural cause, as the individual sins because human nature sinned.   [965

... Impatience. The characteristic note of a baby is its inability to release itself from emotional instincts; he wants everything and cries until he gets it. He cannot endure the tension between need and satisfaction. Adults in whom the law of degeneration operates have exactly the same tension; they cannot endure, for example, the morning paper not arriving for breakfast, or the coffee being cold, or a wait of five minutes at the barbershop.   [966

TERROR

Terror is fear in those who practice terror; it is a dread that seizes a person who is cruel to others.   [967

THEOLOGY

Theology is a science just as much as psychology or physics is. It is really a sad commentary on Universities that they should teach courses in how to swing Indian clubs but none in the science of theology.   [968

THOUGHT

... Action. Thought is the bow, and action is the arrow; thought the seed, and action the fruit; every good archer must have the former, and every good former the latter. Thought and action go together like a piece of artillery; the one takes aim, the other shoots.   [969

... Life. If we do not live as we think, we soon begin to think as we live.   [969-A

... Sin. Our Lord went into the soul, and laid hold of thought, and branded even the *desire* for sin as a sin . . . Evil that can be put into statistics, or that can be locked in jails, is too late to remedy. [970

THOUGHTS

. . . Actions. If our thoughts are bad, our actions will also be bad. The problem of impure actions is basically the problem of impure thoughts; the way to keep a man from robbing a bank is to distract him from thinking about robbing a bank. Political, social, and economic injustices are, first, psychic evils—they originate in the mind. They become social evils because of the intensity of the thought that begot them. [971

. . . Mind. The mind is like a clock that is constantly running down; it has to be wound up daily with good thoughts. [972

TIME

Every moment comes to you pregnant with a divine purpose; time being so precious that God deals it out only second by second. Once it leaves your hands and your power to do with it as you please, it plunges into eternity, to remain forever whatever you made it. [973

. . . Effects. Whenever time on earth is seen as all-important, the elders talk about "the future which is in the hands of the young," everyone is afraid to speak of his age, and the subject of growing old is treated in a manner midway between an insult and a sneer. Like beasts trapped, not in cages but in time, such men become angry with time for passing: the hastening years diminish pleasure and cast a shadow one must try not to see. But since one cannot hope to escape it forever, the fear of death grows apace. It is no accident that the present civilization, which has emphasized sex as no other age in the history of Christianity has emphasized it, lives in constant fear of death. Baudelaire rightly pictured modern love as sitting on a skull. When the flesh is given a moral value, it produces life; when sex frustrates morality, it ends in death. [974

... Eternity. God says to us, "If you give Me your time, I will give you My Eternity." [975

... Now. Every moment brings us more treasures than we can gather. The great value of the now, spiritually viewed, is that it carries a message God has directed personally to us. [976

... Use Of. The time one has for anything depends on how much he values it. Thinking determines the uses of time; time does not rule over thinking. [977

TOLERANCE

Love of God and man, as an ideal, has lately been replaced by the new ideal of tolerance which inspires no sacrifices. Why should any human being in the world be merely tolerated? What man has ever made a sacrifice in the name of tolerance? It leads men, instead, to express their own egotism in a book or a lecture that patronizes the downtrodden group. One of the cruelest things that can happen to a human being is to be tolerated. Never once did our Lord say, "Tolerate your enemies!" But He did say, "Love your enemies; do good to them that hate you." [978

...Indifference. A system of tolerance which reposes upon indifference to truth and morality rather than upon charity and the sacredness of the person, and thus produces on the one hand a national impotency to deal with fifth columnists, because if there is no wrong how can they be wrong, and on the other hand, breeds atheism, anti-religion and anti-Semitism is not worth preserving—Let it perish!

[1979

TOTALITARIANISM

Even though Christ Himself would not deliver the world from the powers of totalitarian states, as He did not deliver Himself, we must see His purpose in it all. Maybe His children are being persecuted by the world in order that they might withdraw themselves from the world; maybe His most violent enemies may be doing His work negatively, for it could be the mission of totalitarianism to preside over the liquidation of a modern world that became indifferent to God and His moral laws. [1980

TRADITION

Nothing is more tragic in an individual who once was wise than to lose his memory, and nothing is more tragic to a civilization than the loss of its tradition. [1981

TRAGEDY

There can never be tragedy where men's conception of life is sordid. One of the essentials of tragedy is a belief in the dignity of human life. And a further condition of all tragedy is immortality. If there is no justice beyond the

246

grave, then tragedy is pointless. Tragedy is something more than pain. [982

TRANSCENDENCE

Transcendence of some kind is required to give meaning to history . . . The instinct for transcendence explains the Messianism of Karl Marx, who secularized it in a coming world order wherein there would be no class but the proletariat. Even here, he transcended the immanent dialectics of history, by positing a regime wherein the dialectic would no longer hold sway. This is one of the basic contradictions of Communism, for why should the dialectics intrinsic to both history and matter, end with a classless society? [983

TRANSFIGURATION

. . . Transcendence. Transcendence not only explains freedom and mastery over nature, but it alone makes possible the transfiguration of this world. Transfiguration is not the same as futurism, which regards this world as becoming better and better until it is turned into an early paradise. Transfiguration means that through catastrophe, crisis, and final judgment, old things are made new. This new kingdom is not in time at all, but in eternity; its existence is not due to an eruption of the mundane with the heavenly, but a visitation of the spiritual with the human—a visitation morally conditioned. It is the very reverse of the Tower of Babel. [984

TRIBULATION

It is the winds and the winters which try the herbs, the flowers, and the trees, and only the strongest survive. So tribulation tries the soul, and in the strong it develops patience, and patience, in its turn, hope, and hope finally begets love. [985

TRUST

We generally trust only those who trust us; that is why there is a special providence for those who trust in God. [986

... Man. We may not safely put our trust in any manmade system or in any man. [987

TRUTH

It is easy to find truth; it is hard to face it, and harder still to follow it. [988

... God. Some psychologists and sociologists like to rap their knuckles at the door of truth about mankind, but they would run away if the door ever opened, showing man's contingency on God. The only people who ever arrive at a knowledge of God are those who, when the door is opened, accept that Truth and shoulder the responsibilities it brings. [989

... Information. There is a world of difference between a mind that has in it ten thousand bits of uncorrelated information, and a mind that is like an organism in which one fact or truth is functionally related to every other truth, as the heart is related to the legs and arms. [990

... Natural; Divine. Natural truths must be known in order to be loved, but divine truths must be loved in order to be fully known. One cannot love music unless he knows it, but the more one loves it the better it is understood.   [991

... **Responsibility.** Truth brings with it great responsibilities; that is why so many men keep their hands open to welcome it, but never close them to grasp it . . . in their cowardice, they keep their minds "open" so they will never have to close on anything that would entail responsibility, duty, moral correction or altered behavior.   [992

·· U ··

UNITED NATIONS

The various nations that constitute the United Nations can ultimately be united only by something outside of themselves . . . something that has priority over each of them, and to which they must submit even when it goes against them . . . Heaven knows that if we do not obey our own politicians, we will not obey someone else's. First there is glory to God in the Highest, then there is peace on earth.

[993

UNITY

. . . Spirit.   One person is unable to be completely united with another because *matter is the basis of impenetrability or division; spirit is the basis of unity*. We come close to unity because of our spirit; we are precluded from it because we are physical as well as spiritual beings. This does not mean to say that body-love is incompatible with soul-love, for in marriage the first is the condition of the second. It only means that the ideal unity which body-love seeks to attain never is completely realized as an abiding and permanent thing.

[994

UNIVERSE

... Relation to God. The problem of the relation of the universe to God admits of two extreme and erroneous views, both of which have had their day of philosophical inquiry. The one extreme is deism, which divorces God from the universe. The other extreme is pantheism which identifies God with the universe . . . Deism, at the present time, is an unpopular philosophy and perhaps even a dead one. Pantheism is equally unpopular as a word, but not as a system, for it dominates practically all religious thinking today.   [995

UNIVERSITIES

There are very few universities in the world; there are many "pluriversities." The university is not just a body of students gathered in one place; it is a unified body of knowledge, a common pool of principles which all accept and know . . . How often it happens that courses in philosophy, for example, are nothing but histories of philosophical systems. If architecture were taught that way, no one would ever be prepared to build a house; he would only know how houses had been built in different periods of history.   [996

... Philosophy. When a university or a college loses its philosophy of life, and its reason for educating, it breaks up into departments and becomes a crazy quilt of unrelated information like a glorified quiz program.   [997

UNSELFISHNESS

As the bird that sings for others gladdens its own heart with song . . . as the sun burns itself out to light a world, so does everything—man included—become good by doing good to others.   [998

VALUES

... **Moral.** When a teacher or parent lacks values which command respect, disobedience automatically increases. Juvenile delinquency rises in direct ratio to the decline of moral values among parents. [999

... **Other Nations.** We don't seem to understand that some people of the world want things other than our high standard of living; that a German, for example, might want an encyclopedia instead of a $300 deep freezer. [1000

VANITY

... **Argument.** Vain people like to prove themselves right, especially in argument. What is important is not the *truth* of things, but their being *right*. [1001

... **Giving.** Why is it that beggars always use tin cups? It is because they appeal to the vanity of the giver who likes to hear the clink of the coin in the cup. [1002

... **Modern.** The modern man's desire to serve the best liquor, his woman's ambition to be the best dressed, the college sophomore's hope of being the most studiously un-kempt—these are symptoms of an egotistical vanity which makes its owners dread not being noticed.   [1003

VICTORIANS

... **Sex.** The Victorians wrote about love as if sex were never involved. Even the body was clothed with yards and yards of bottle green, carrot red, brown and dirty ocher; human beings reached a point where they had as many coats as onions. Men wore beards which covered their faces and necks. It was an era in which many wished to be free from all mention of sex, unless it was sin in another.   [1004

VIRGIN BIRTH

He who believes that Our Lord is true God and true man never is troubled by the Virgin Birth.   [1005

VIRTUE

... **Salvation.** Even when the will is perverse—even when a creature is enthralled and captivated by one great sinful adhesion, which makes his days a flight from God toward lust or power—even then there are some few good and commendable acts which contradict his general attitude. These isolated acts of virtue are like a clean handle on a dirty bucket; with them, God can lift a soul to His Peace.   [1006

··W··

WAR

War is not necessary, but it does become an inseparable ailment of any world that abandons the supremacy of the spirit. In any era of history where politics is the major interest, war is the major consequence. [1007

It used to be that wars were hard to wage, that peace came naturally with victory. Today the situation is reversed; the powers of destruction are greater than the powers of construction in the modern world. [1008

... Atomic. War, up to this point, was a means to an end. An atomic war would be the end! [1009

... Inner. There is an illusion abroad that war is always wrong and that the world should be free from war. This is false. There must always be war, but the war should not be on the outside; it should be on the inside. As we war against the evil within us, the wars on the outside decrease. The reason we happen to live in a century of wars is because we have neglected to wage battle against the forces that destroy the mind and the soul. He who does not find the enemy within will find the enemy without. [1010

254

... **Mothers.** A tiny ball of unconsciousness needs much mother care to become all that God destined it to be. Maybe that is why mothers are against war; they realize better than anyone else how long it takes to make a man.   [1011

... **Politics; Religion.** The problem is ever the same; the invasion of the spiritual by the political. If it be objected that religion once made Henry come to Canossa, let it be stated that it was for exactly the same reason that the world made war against Hitler, namely because of his usurpation of spiritual freedom. The difference between Henry's time and Hitler's is that when religion had some influence in the world and kings had consciences, it was possible for the church to inspire them to penance.   [1012

... **Selfishness; Wickedness.** Wars are not caused solely by aggression or tyranny from without, for unless there had been the spirit of selfishness in some minds there could never be aggression. Nothing ever happens in the world that does not happen first inside human hearts. War is actually a projection of our own wickedness; our forgetfulness of God has more to do with war than is generally believed.   [1013

... **Today.** Wars today are total. Probably the last war between gentlemen was the Civil War. War is now a struggle for survival. The planet can be disturbed, and even future generations made physically and mentally defective through atomic radiation. At the end of an atomic war, there will be no peace conference; we will just gather up the broken pieces.   [1014

. . . World. Two world wars have not made the world better, but worse. And one wonders if the next catastrophe will be a war in the same sense of the last two or rather some calamity more surely calculated to produce repentance in man. [1015

WEAKNESS

. . . Western World. Our weakness in the Western world is, not being sure that anything is true. We are much like Pilate when Our Lord said to him, "I have come to give testimony of the truth and those who are of the truth heareth My voice." Pilate sneered, "What is truth?" and then turned his back on it. His pragmatic training had led him to believe that mere expediency and not principle was the right philosophy of life. [1016

WEALTH

. . . Goodness. People begin to believe that, because they are rich on the outside, they are good on the inside. This extreme is known as avarice, though it passes today under the polite name of security. [1017

. . . Happiness. Does happiness consist of riches or wealth? There are indeed many advantages to riches . . . But wealth can never constitute happiness, because it is only a means to happiness and extrinsic to oneself . . . If you put a penny close enough to your eye, you can shut out the light of the sun. [1018

. . . Riches. No one has the right to despise the rich until, like Our Lord, he has proven himself free from the passion to possess . . . and then he will not wish to despise any one. [1019

WICKEDNESS

. . . Totality. When a germ gets into the blood stream, it does not isolate itself in the right arm and spare the left; it is the whole body that is stricken. So with humanity. Being one body, everyone who belongs to our race is sinful to some degree. It is *our* wicked world, not *theirs.* It is not the Communists alone who are the cause of the world's ills, for every idea in Communism originated in our Western World. All of us stand in need of redemption. [1020

WILL

. . . Act Of. An act of the will is vital to any accomplishment. Doctors tell us that nothing is a greater help to the sick man than a will to live. So if we are to overcome our vices, we must bring a strong will to bear on them . . . After the Prodigal had entered into himself and left the environment of sin, his next step was to brace himself with the great resolve, "I will arise and go to my father." [1021

. . . Love. Evil habits cannot be overcome by the will alone: love is required as well. No alcoholic is cured until he finds something to value more highly than the attractions of alcohol. No other evil is renounced until the sinner finds some positive good he prizes above his sin. Our Lord warned us of the house, swept and garnished, which was filled by seven devils worse than the first; this was the inevitable result when an evil was driven out and no good was sent to take its place. [1022

WILL OF GOD

We must do everything within our power to fulfill God's will as it is made known to us by His Mystical Body, the Commandments and our lawfully constituted superiors, and the duties flowing from our state in life. Everything that is outside our power, we must abandon and surrender to His Holy Will. [1023

... **Success; Failure.** We must not think that God is good because we have a fat bank account. Providence is not the Provident Loan. Sanctity consists in accepting whatever happens to us as God's will, and even thanking Him for it. [1024

WINE

... **Use.** To see no difference in wine when it is used for intoxication and when it is used for consecration, means that a man is blind enough not to see any difference in a rope when it is employed to hold up a man's trousers, and when it is used to hold up his neck. [1025

WISDOM

... **Facts.** Facts as such are nothing; an imbecile can pass his life with a wise man and not be any wiser. [1026

... **Science.** The regeneration of society requires that a distinction be made between science and wisdom. Science is concerned with means or techniques; wisdom is concerned with goals, destinies, and purposes. A mechanical civilization is built on science; a cultural, on goals or destinies. [1027

WOMAN

...**Love.** A woman never tells why she loves; she just tells you *how* she loves. [1027-A

...**Man.** The first difference between a man and a woman is that a man is concerned principally with *things* and a woman with *persons*. [1028

WOMANHOOD

...**Civilizations.** To a great extent the level of any civilization is the level of its womanhood. When a man loves a woman, he has to become worthy of her. The higher her virtue, the more noble her character, the more devoted she is to truth, justice, and goodness, the more a man has to aspire to be worthy of her. The history of civilization could actually be written in terms of the *level of its women*. [1029

WOMEN

...**Anger.** A woman gets angry when a man denies his faults, because she knew them all along. His lying mocks her affection; it is the deceit that angers her more than the faults. [1030

...**Catty.** How do some women know that other women are catty, unless they themselves know how it feels to be catty. [1031

...**"Double Standard".** The so-called "double standard," which does not exist and which has no ethical foundation, is actually based on the unconscious impulse of man to

regard women as the preservers of ideals, even when he fails
to live up to them.   [1032

... **Equality.** Modern woman has been made equal with
man, but she has not been made happy.   [1033

... **Femininity.** It is not doing man's work in business
which harms woman; it is doing it in man's way rather than
a woman's which is apt to harm her. As Dr. Jung said, "In
taking up a masculine calling, studying and working in a
man's way, woman is doing something not wholly in agree-
ment with her feminine nature." The woman's outstanding
characteristic is that she can do everything for the love of a
man, but those women who can achieve for the love of a
thing are most exceptional, because this does not really agree
with their natures. The love of a thing is man's prerog-
ative.   [1034

... **Love.** When a woman's love becomes venal, everything is lost. When it is kept noble, it brings to the world the
balm of tenderness and devotion. The level of any civilization is thus the level of its womanhood.   [1035

... **Mothers.** Motherhood becomes a kind of priesthood.
She brings God to man by preparing the flesh in which the
soul will be implanted; she brings man to God in offering the
child back again to the Creator.   [1036

... **Religion.** The oft-repeated suggestion that woman is
more religious than man has some basis in truth, but only in
the sense that her nature is more readily disposed toward the

ideal. The woman has a greater measure of the eternal and man a greater measure of time, but both are essential for an incarnational universe, in which eternity embraces time in a stable of Bethlehem. [1037

... **Vice.** When there is descent into an equal degree of vice, there is always a greater scandal caused by a woman than the man. [1038

WORDS

The spoken word is like the spent arrow; it cannot be recalled in its flight but its responsibilities endure forever . . . a kind word gives encouragement to the despondent heart, and a cruel word makes others sob their way to the grave. [1039

WORK

... **Activity.** There is so much stress put upon work and activity that our economic system has almost degenerated to a point where we go to work to get cash, in order to buy food, in order to get the strength, in order to go to work again. [1040

... **Love.** No work is hard where there is love. [1041

WORLD

... **Dimensions.** Forgetting God, man's vision has lately been reduced to a single dimension; he now thinks of his activity as limited to the surface of the earth—a plane whereon he moves not up to God or down to Satan, but only to the right or to the left. [1042

. . . End Of. Death has unexpectedly become a phenomenon that not only the person must face, but society or civilization itself. [1043

. . . Freudian. Let anyone come into a Freudian world and say, "Blessed are the clean of heart" and he will be crucified. [1044

. . . God. When Our Blessed Lord spoke of His doctrine as a yoke, He asked His followers to be pure in a world full of Freudians; to be poor in spirit in a world of competitive capitalism; to be meek amidst the armament makers; to mourn among the pleasure seekers; to hunger and thirst after justice amidst the pragmatists; to be merciful among those who would seek revenge. Anyone who does these things will be hated by a world that does not want God. [1045

. . . Love. Our Lord never said it was wrong to love the world; He said only that it was a loss, for "what shall a man give in exchange for his soul?" . . . Sanctity, then, is not giving up the world. It is exchanging the world. It is a continuation of that sublime transaction of the Incarnation in which Christ said to man: "You give Me your humanity, I will give you My divinity. You give Me your time, I will give you My eternity. You give Me your bonds, I will give you My omnipotence. You give Me your slavery, I will give you My freedom. You give Me your death, I will give you My life. You give Me your nothingness, I will give you My all." [1046

. . . Man. A boy was asked by his father to work out a jigsaw puzzle which was a map of the world. In an amazingly short time, the jigsaw puzzle was put together. The father said, "How did you know how to put this puzzle together? You do not know geography." The little boy answered, "On the other side was the puzzle of a man. So I put the man together, and the world came out all right."   [1047

...Orthodoxy. It is easy to be a "pink" in this century, as it was easy to be a "liberal" in the nineteenth; it is easy to be a "materialist" today, as it was easy to be an "idealist" in the nineteenth century, but to keep one's head in the midst of all these changing moods and fancies, so that one is right, not when the world is right, but right when the world is wrong, is the thrill of a tight-rope walker, the thrill of the romance of orthodoxy.   [1048

...Problems. If the troubles of our world are outside of us—socially and economically—we shall have to submit to a cruel fate indeed. If the trouble with the world lies inside the human heart, then it is possible to remedy all that trouble. We can remedy it by returning again to the great tradition of our Founding Fathers, of being once more a religious people, loving our neighbor, our country, and serving God.   [1049

...Sex; Purity. While the world says: "Blessed is sex," the Beatitude teaches: "Blessed are the clean of heart."   [1050

...Tragedy. The tragedy of today is that the world is not only tearing up the photographs of a good society, but also tearing up the negatives.   [1051

WORLD RELIGIONS

... Christianity. Below the superficial resemblances between Christianity and other world religions, one sees radical and fundamental differences. The remarkable thing is that being so much like other religions, the Christian religion should be so very different . . . To ignore the differences behind the resemblances and to say that Christianity was produced by the same cause as other religions is a trick of lead logic, akin to saying that because the thousands of paintings in the Louvre are similar, inasmuch as they all contain red, white, and blue colors, then, they were all painted by the same artist. [1052

... World. The world today is no longer deciding which of the Christian religions is true, but which of the world religions is most useful. Some even say that all these religions are passing phases of religion. [1053

WORLDLINESS

The Sermon on the Mount is so much at variance with all that our world holds dear that the world will crucify anyone who tries to live up to its values. Because Christ preached them, He had to die. [1054

WORRY

... Atheism. All worry is atheism, because it is a want of trust in God. [1055

... Tension. It is a medical fact that tense and worried people have more accidents resulting in fractures than those who have a clear conscience and a divine goal in life. Some men and women complain that they "never get a break," that the world is their enemy, that they have "bad luck." A person resigned to God's holy will utters no such complaint; whatever comes along, he welcomes it.   [1056

WORSHIP

Worship must take its character from the Nature of God, and not from the nature of any people or nation or race. Almost all attempts at religious unity start with man instead of with God the Father. All who are looking for the unity of religion must not start whittling away the Divine Truths.   [1057

...**Duty.** You have a duty to worship God, not because He will pout and be imperfect and unhappy if you do not, but because if you do not worship God you will be imperfect and unhappy.   [1058

WRATH

...**God.** God seems Wrath only to those who refuse to make use of His Forgiveness.   [1059

WRITING

...**Modern.** Modern writing is made up of experiences strung together, but leading nowhere, nor painting any moral. Minds never inquire where they came from, or where they are going; they are just on the way. They never begin, they never develop, they never end—they just stop. Nothing links things together except more succession in time; the needle of writing is drawn through the cloth but it weaves no pattern.   [1060

··Y··

YOUTH

...**Hero Worship.** Hardly strong enough to stand on his own amorous feet, a youth has to lean on somebody else. Hero worship is very strong; very often the hero is a player of the drums, or a celluloid phantom, or a moaning singer. The nobler the hero, the nobler the character which will unfold in later life. [1061

...**Jaded.** Jaded youths are constantly in search of a thrill, whether it be alcohol, marijuana cigarettes, or even murder . . . Already jaded in infancy by having everything that they wanted, they become tired of their satiated emotions as they seek for new thrills to satisfy their sickened egos. [1062

...**Listening.** Youth must learn to listen before it speaks, as the wheat must absorb before it can produce the grain. [1063

...**Maturity.** Youth grows to maturity like wheat in a field. Wheat is healthy when rooted in the soil and in communion with the sky. Youth is normal when rooted in the family and in communion with the invisible forces that make the soul. Take the grain of wheat out of that field before it is ripe, and it acquires a false independence which withers it to death. [1064

...Pampered. Those who are pampered during youth . . . retain a delusion of grandeur during life and are very subject to physical and mental breakdowns. [1065

...Potential. There is a hidden potential for sacrifice in modern youth which has not been tapped. They are prepared for far greater self-discipline than the educators and elders have given them; they are like soldiers ready for battle, but lacking generals. [1066

...Privacy. When we are children, mothers get hold of our noses with the injunction, "Blow hard." A day finally comes in the life of every boy when he resents it; on the day he can say, "Today, I am a man." When he objects to the intrusion of his privacy, he comes to a recognition that he is a personality and that there are certain inviolable rights associated with it. [1067

...The Church. A young man goes to college. He could there join an Oriental Sun cult, or become a Buddhist, or a Confucianist, or start a new religion of his own, and his parents would probably only remonstrate; but let him join the Church and there would be war! [1068

...Training. The error of the Western world is to train youth in love without discipline; the error of Communism is to train youth in discipline without love. [1069

··Z··

ZEAL

...Lack Of.   There are no longer any deep loves or
passionate devotions to great causes; expediency and self-
interest are too general. Politics and economics are our major
interests, and neither can warm the souls of men. Our fires
of patriotism, evangelization, and zeal are being reduced to
embers. We are cold, dull, and apathetic. One tiny effect of
that want of fire is the fact that in our Western world there
are but few orators. Most men in public life are readers.

[1070

THE WIT OF
FULTON J. SHEEN

I see you are back to have your faith lifted!

. . .

A six-year-old girl, anxious to help The Society for the Propagation of The Faith, put up a sign on her front lawn: "lemonade—5¢ a glass." Many customers came back three and four times and soon the lemonade was gone. Her mother asked her where she was getting all the lemons. The little girl answered, "from the cocktail shaker you had in the icebox."

. . .

When you are getting kicked from the rear it means that you are out in front.

. . .

If you copy anything out of one book, it is plagiarism. If you copy it out of two books, it is research. If you copy it out of six books, you are a professor.

. . .

There is nothing that develops character like a pat on the back, provided it is given often enough, hard enough and— low enough.

. . .

A denial of guilt is a denial of responsibility, and a denial of responsibility is a denial of freedom. Illustrating . . . is a cartoon in which a psychoanalyst is pictured telling a Mother: "Yes, your boy is stubborn, cruel, perverted, a kleptomaniac, has criminal tendencies—but bad, no."

. . .

Recently, on the subway, I got up and gave my seat to a lady who was holding on to a strap. She was rather surprised and said to me, "Why did you do that?" Seeing that she was incapable of understanding a spiritual reason, I said to her, "Madame, I tell you, ever since I was a little boy, I have had an infinite respect for a woman with a strap in her hand."

. . .

There is a difference between blarney and baloney. Blarney is the varnished truth; baloney is the unvarnished lie.

. . .

A little girl went to her daddy once and said, "Daddy, are you afraid of cows?"

"No."

"Are you afraid of snakes?"

"No."

"Are you afraid of long woolly worms?"

"No."

"Daddy, you aren't afraid of anything but Mama, are you?"

. . .

The best definition of an adult that was ever given is that an adult is one who has stopped growing at both ends and has begun to grow in the middle.

. . .

I remember once I was to meet a man by the name of Lummock. My secretary said, "Now, remember that his name rhymes with 'stomach.' " Do you know what I called him?—Kelly!

. . .

An old Irish lady, watching a bishop read his sermon, once said, "If he can't remember it, how does he expect us to?"

. . .

History? The British never remember it; the Irish never forget it; the Russians never make it, and the Americans never learn from it.

. . .

Two Americans visiting Switzerland were discussing Europe. One of the Americans rather cynically said that there was nothing beautiful in Europe: "Cathedrals are old and dusty; the castles are without bathrooms; the art is not beautiful, for the most part it is religious art, having none of the squares and circles that you find in our progressive American art; there is nothing beautiful in Europe." His compatriot, pointing to the Alps, said, "But don't you think Switzerland is beautiful?" His answer was, "Take away the scenery and what have you got left?"

. . .

The Soviet concept of peace reminds one of the man who importuned his friend, saying, "You say you are a lover of peace, Casey; then why did you throw the brick at Murphy?" Casey said, "Because he was very peaceful after I threw it."

. . .

Blarney is always associated with imagination, which also seems a peculiar quality of the Irish. Those of you who have ever been down to Killarney probably met the boatmen there. Once I asked, "Is Killarney deep?"

"Deep? I had a nephew that dove in there six months ago. We got a post card from him in Australia last week. He wants his winter underwear."

. . .

I know one mother who locked herself in the playpen; it was the only way she could ever get peace.

. . .

There was a preacher once who was saying to the congregation, "It is wrong to steal horses." The congregation answered, "Amen, amen." "It is wrong to steal cows." "Amen! Amen!" Then he said, "It is wrong to steal chickens." And someone shouted back, "Now he is meddling!"

. . .

Every unlikable person is an "I" specialist.

. . .

Many a boasting self-made man is a beautiful example of unskilled labor. One thing, however, that must be said to his credit is that he relieves the Lord of a terrific amount of responsibility.

. . .

A fat woman went to a gymnasium. The instructor said she would have to chin herself twenty times a day. She asked, "Which chin?"

. . .

Ed Wynn was once talking to someone who boasted that he knew operas very well. Ed Wynn struck one note on the piano and said, "If you know operas so well, from what opera does that note come?"

. . .

A woman once told Dr. Johnson when he was preparing his dictionary, "I am so glad there are no impure words in your dictionary." Doctor Johnson answered, "How did you know? Did you look for them?"

. . .

We know of a wife who said that during a year and a half of her marriage to an alcoholic she never once saw him take a drink, but never once did he draw a sober breath. It was only after a year and a half that she discovered how he procured his alcohol. He had one room of the house in which there were thirty or forty loving cups mounted on the wall. He hired someone during the night to fill all those cups with liquor. During the daytime as he would pass rapidly from one room to another, he would suddenly jump on a chair, empty a loving cup, and then pass on—and pass out.

. . .

Some athletes are good students, but those who devote themselves to the training of the body generally are not conspicuous intellectually. I heard of a college that was planning to have three football teams: one for offense, the other for defense, and the third to attend classes.

. . .

A child psychologist has been defined as one who would never strike a child—except in self-defense.

. . .

One morning, a husband was about to go to work and his wife said, "John, I wish you would go into the kitchen and give Hilda a good talking to." The husband said, "How's that? I thought you were very satisfied with her." The wife said, "So I am, but she is beating the carpets today, and she always does it better when she is angry."

• • •

The woman who was suing for higher alimony . . . told the judge that she needed twenty-four new dresses a month. The judge said to her, "What could a woman possibly want with twenty-four new dresses?"

Her answer was, "Twenty-four new hats."

• • •

The other day I was in an elevator in a department store. I was shopping on the fifth floor, and I wanted to go to the sixth. I stepped into the elevator and several other passengers entered at the same time. Just as the elevator was about to start, the operator said, "Going up." Some woman rushed out madly saying, "I don't want to go up; I want to go down." Then turning to me—I do not know why she picked on me—she said, "I did not think I could go wrong following you." I said, "Madam, I only take people *up*, not down."

• • •

A mother one day said to a school teacher, "I know Reginald has been throwing inkwells out of the window, and throwing spitballs at you, but under no consideration spank Reginald. It will give him a guilt complex. Just hit the boy in front of him, and it will frighten Reginald."

• • •

A little girl was always lying. She was given a St. Bernard dog . . . This little girl went out and told all the neighbors that she had been given a lion. The mother called her and said, "I told you not to lie. You go upstairs and tell God you are sorry. Promise God you will not lie again."

She went upstairs and said her prayers and then came down. Her mother said, "Did you tell God you are sorry?"

The little girl said, "Yes, I did. And God said that some times He finds it hard to tell a dog from a lion, too."

. . .

A prune has been defined as a worried plum.

. . .

A lawyer who was arguing at great length before the judge, presenting one precedent after another . . . felt that he was getting a little too deep and confusing for the judge; so he inquired of the judge, "Your Honor, are you following me?"

The judge said, "I follow you all right, but if I knew the way back, I would leave you now."

. . .

A tramp came to a farmer one day and asked for a little work. The farmer said, "You go down to the basement. There you will find a number of potatoes. I want you to put them into three piles. Put all of the good ones in one pile, all of the bad ones in another pile, and then in the middle, you can put those that are just half good and half bad."

About an hour later the tramp said to the farmer, "I don't want the job. It drives me crazy making decisions."

. . .

I always like the little girl who said one day to her mother, when the cat was purring, "The cat went to sleep and left its engine running."

277

• • •

There is a story of an unfortunate monk who was admonished by his abbot for coming in late for chapel every morning. "We must put a stop to this," the abbot told the monk. "Tomorrow morning when you hear the bell I want you to imagine that you are engulfed in the fires and torment of purgatory. I guarantee you will jump out of bed."

Next morning the poor monk was as late as ever. "What happened?" the abbot asked him later. "Didn't you follow my suggestion?"

"Yes, I did," the monk replied, "but I decided I liked it down there."

• • •

Some time ago we received a letter from a mother who named her baby Fulton. Fulton is now four years of age. One day the mother looked for him; she shouted and screamed, but no answer. Finally, the mother went to the garret; there she found the little boy dressed up, with coat, hat and a suitcase in his hand.

She said, "Where are you going, Fulton?" He said, "I am going to New York to see Bishop Sheen. I was named after him." The mother asked, "What have you got in the suitcase?" He said, "My little sister. She is going, too."

• • •

If you just put your head between your hands today to think out something, you are asked if you have a headache.

• • •

Did you know that, in Heaven, an angel is a no-body?

• • •

It seems that within the last few weeks, the Murphy family was watching TV upstairs. A robber came in and took about three hundred dollars in cash and a couple of thousand dollars in jewels.

The next day one of the robbers phoned and said, "We found out that we were in the wrong house. We are very sorry; we sure did have butterflies in our stomach when we saw Bishop Sheen on television."

Apparently, that is the only effect we have—we create butterflies in stomachs. We apparently did not disturb their consciences or induce them to return the stolen goods.

· · ·

I heard of a wife who got even with her husband. He said, "Dear, there's an old-clothesman at the door." She answered, "Tell him I have all I need."

· · ·

There is a story—and it is only a story—about a man who went to confession. During confession he stole the priest's watch. He then told the priest that he had stolen a watch. The priest said: "You must make restitution." The thief said: "I will give it to you, Father." "No," said the priest, "give it to the owner," The penitent then said: "The owner won't take it back." "In that case," said the priest, "you can keep it."

· · ·

Everyone remembers the Fourth of July orator who tried to talk without any notes, until he said that we all ought to be grateful to the "One from Whom our rights and liberties descended." He reached into his pocket, pulled out his notes and then added: "Almighty God."

· · ·

An eternally feminine problem is always: "What will I wear?" It probably began the day after the initial rebellion, when Eve looked up at the leaves of the fig tree and said: "I wonder which one I will wear today?"

• • •

If you tell a citizen of Erin it is a bad day, nine times out of ten he will answer: "It's a good day to save your soul."

• • •

I heard of a woman who had seven cats. She had seven holes cut in every door in the house. Asked the reason, she said, "When I say 'Scat!' *I mean it.*"

• • •

Some probably believe the reason why Cain turned out so badly was because Eve had no books on child psychology.

• • •

I was talking in Syracuse where they had built a tremendously large armory. A couple of the ushers were discussing the coming wrestling matches, the boxing matches, roller skating, prize fights, and so forth, and one of the ushers said, "I think we'll have a big crowd next Thursday night. We'll fill the place."

Another usher asked him, "Who's coming?"

Another usher said, "Bishop Sheen."

"Who does he wrestle?"

• • •

Specialization has reached such a state today that patients have to learn to diagnose themselves before they know which specialist to call.

• • •

This is the oldest story in the world about women. Therefore, like wine, treat it with respect.

After the Fall in the Garden of Eden, Adam was out walking with his two boys, Cain and Abel. They passed by the wrecked ruins of the once beautiful Garden of Paradise, and Adam pulled the two boys to him and looked in and said, "Boys, that's where your mother ate us out of house and home."

• • •

Shortly after my appointment as bishop, I was to appear on a TV show. I arrived a few minutes early at the studio, so I stepped into a drug store for a cup of coffee, not having time enough, however, to remove the red cape in which I was to appear on the telecast. The girl at the counter was serving customers a-mile-a-minute. Finally she turned to me:

"And what's yours, Cock Robin?"

• • •

The six-year-old moppet of a writer we know was playing with several other small fry. All the others had make-shift capes slung over their shoulders and were running around wildly shouting, "Watch out, I'm Superman!"

The little girl watched them critically for a few minutes, then called a halt.

"I'm not allowed to watch Superman," she announced. "Let's play Bishop Sheen."

• • •

Two Irishmen, Murphy and Kelly, were bitter rivals. An angel was sent to pacify Murphy. "You are very bitter and cold and cruel toward Kelly; to cure you, the Good Lord has promised to give you one of anything in the world if you will only let Kelly have two of them."

"If I am head of one labor union," Murphy said, "does that mean Kelly will be head of two?"

"Yes," said the angel.

"If I win the Irish Sweepstakes once, Kelly wins twice?"
The angel said, "That's right."

"And if I have a brass band following me, Kelly has two?"
"Yes."

Murphy said, "Angel, I'll take a glass eye."

• • •

Socialism is that part of the economic system under which
the state imposes a heavy tax on all the God-given teeth to
supply every one with state-given teeth, whether they are
needed or not, and then rations everything that can be
chewed.

• • •

An astronomer once remarked to me: "To an astronomer,
man is nothing but an infinitesimal dot in an infinite universe."

An interesting point of view, but he seems to forget that
the infinitesimal dot of a man is still the astronomer.

• • •

I'm sorry that some of you have to stand for this talk. I
include those who are seated.

• • •

An atheist is a man who has no invisible means of support.

• • •

I feel it is time that I also pay tribute to my four writers,
Matthew, Mark, Luke, and John.

Biography (Vita)

SHEEN, the Most Rev. FULTON J(OHN)
50 Chestnut Street,
Rochester, New York

BASIC INFORMATION

Born: El Paso, Illinois, May 8, 1895; Ordained, 1919; Papal Chamberlain, 1934; Domestic Prelate, 1935; National Director, SPOF, 1950–66; Appointed Bishop: Pius XII, 1951; Auxiliary Bishop of New York, 1951–66; Appointed to Vatican II, Commission on the Missions by Pope John XXIII, 1962; Appointed to Post-Conciliar Commission on the Missions by Pope Paul VI, 1965; Consecrated Missionary Bishops with Pope John XXIII in St. Peter's Rome, 1966; Appointed Bishop of Rochester, New York, by Pope Paul VI, 1966; Elected by the American Episcopacy to the first Committee for the Propagation of the Faith, 1966; Appointed by the American Episcopacy to the first administrative Committee of the National Council of Catholic Bishops, 1966–67.

DEGREES

J.C.B., Catholic U. of America, 1920; Ph.D., Louvain, Belgium, 1923; S.T.D., Rome, 1924; Agrégé en philosophie, Louvain, 1925; Honorary: LL.D., Litt.D., L.H.D.

EDUCATOR

Dogmatic Theology Prof., St. Edmund's College, Ware, England, 1925; Philosophy Prof., Catholic U. of America, 1926–50.

PREACHER

Summer conferences, Westminster, London, 1925, 1928, 1931; Catholic Summer School, Cambridge U., 1930–1931; Annual Broadcasts, The Catholic Hour, 1930–1952; Annual Telecasts, 1952 to present.

EDITOR

Worldmission and *Mission* magazines.

COLUMNIST

"God Loves You," Catholic Press; "Bishop Sheen Speaks," Secular Press.

AUTHOR

God and Intelligence, 1925; *Religion Without God,* 1928: *The Life of All Living,* 1929: *The Divine Romance,* 1930; *Old Errors and New Labels,* 1931; *Moods and Truths,* 1932; *Way of the Cross,* 1932; *Seven Last Words,* 1933; *Hymn of the Conquered,* 1933; *The Eternal Galilean,* 1934; *Philosophy of Science,* 1934; *The Mystical Body of Christ,* 1935; *Calvary and the Mass,* 1936; *The Moral Universe,* 1936; *The Cross and the Beatitudes,* 1937; *The Cross and the Crisis,* 1938; *Liberty, Equality and Fraternity*, 1938; *The Rainbow of Sorrow*, 1938; *Victory Over Vice*, 1939; *Whence Come Wars*, 1940; *The Seven Virtues*, 1940; *For God and Country*, 1941; *A Declaration of Dependence*, 1941; *God and War and Peace*, 1942; *The Divine Verdict*, 1943; *The Armor of God*, 1943; *Philosophies at War*, 1943; *Seven Words to the Cross*, 1944; *Seven Pillars of Peace*, 1944; *Love One Another*, 1944; *Seven Words of Jesus and Mary*, 1945; *Preface to Religion*, 1946; *Characters of the Passion*, 1946; *Jesus, Son of Mary*, 1947; *Communism and the Conscience of the West*, 1948; *Philosophy of Religion*, 1948; *Peace of Soul*, 1949; *Lift Up Your Heart*, 1950; *Three to Get Married*, 1951; *The World's First Love*, 1952; *Life Is Worth Living*, Vol. I, 1953; *Life Is Worth Living*, Vol. II, 1954; *The Life of Christ*, 1954; *Way to Happiness*, 1954; *Way to Inner Peace*, 1954; *God Love You*, 1955; *Thinking Life Through*, 1955; *Thoughts for Daily Living*, 1955; *Life Is Worth Living*, Vol. III, 1955; *Life Is Worth Living*, Vol. IV, 1956; *Life Is Worth Living*, Vol. V, 1957; *Life of Christ*, 1958; *This Is the Mass*, 1958; *This Is Rome*, 1960; *Go to Heaven*, 1960; *This Is the Holy Land*, 1961; *These Are the Sacraments*, 1962; *The Priest Is Not His Own*, 1963; *Missions and the World Crisis*, 1964; *The Power of Love*, 1965; *This Is the Mass* (rev. ed.), 1965; *Walk with God*, 1965; *Christmas Inspirations*, 1966; *Footprints in a Darkened Forest*, *Guide to Contentment*, *Easter Inspirations*, *The Quotable Fulton J. Sheen*, 1967.

BISHOP OF ROCHESTER, NEW YORK

On October 26, 1966 Pope Paul VI appointed Bishop Sheen the Bishop of Rochester, New York. The Bishop was installed as Bishop of Rochester on December 15, 1966. From 1950 until that time the bishop was national director for the Holy Father's Society for the Propagation of the Faith which, according to the Pope, is the Church's *principal* mission organization. Bishop

Sheen resigned his professorship of philosophy at the Catholic University of America in 1950, where he had taught for over 23 years.

The Bishop was born in El Paso, Illinois, May 8, 1895, one of four sons of Newton Morris and Delia (Fulton) Sheen. Baptized Peter, he took the name of John at Confirmation and later adopted his mother's maiden name. His father, of Irish ancestry, was a farmer "with an inventive turn of mind." While Fulton was still a small child, the family moved to Peoria, Illinois, where his uncle, Daniel Sheen, a law partner of Robert G. Ingersoll, the famous agnostic, had served as representative in the State Congress.

After attending St. Mary's School, he entered Spalding Institute, a secondary school in Peoria conducted by the Brothers of Mary, from which he graduated in 1913. For his A.B. and M.A. degrees, he went to St. Viator College, Bourbonnais, Illinois, where he was on the debating team (which defeated Notre Dame for the first time) and editorial staff of the college newspaper. Having completed his theological studies, both at St. Viator and at St. Paul's Seminary, St. Paul, Minnesota, he was ordained to the priesthood for the Diocese of Peoria, September 20, 1919.

Obtaining both his S.T.B. and J.C.B. degrees from the Catholic University of America in 1920, he went to the University of Louvain, Belgium, which awarded him his Ph.D. degree three years later. He also attended the Sorbonne in Paris and the Collegio Angelico in Rome. In 1924, he received his S.T.D. degree in Rome. In 1925, while a teacher of dogmatic theology at St. Edmund's College near Ware, England, he was made an Agrégé en Philosophie by Louvain and given the university's Cardinal Mercier International Philosophy Award.

Returning to the United States, he served as a curate of St. Patrick's Church in Peoria; but by the end of 1926 he had joined the Catholic University of America faculty as a philosophy of religion instructor, later being promoted to associate and full professor of philosophy.

He preached at the summer conferences held at Westminster Cathedral in London in 1925 and again from 1928 to 1931; he lectured at the Catholic Summer School at Cambridge University in 1930 and 1931. For five Lenten seasons he preached Sunday evenings at the Paulist Church, New York City, and for many years was annual Lenten preacher at New York's St. Patrick's Cathedral.

In June, 1934, he was appointed Papal Chamberlain—Very Reverend Monsignor, elevated the following year to Domestic Prelate—Right Reverend Monsignor; and on June 11, 1951, he was consecrated Bishop in the Church of Saints John and Paul in Rome by his Eminence, Adeodato Giovanni Cardinal Piazza, secretary of the Sacred Consistorial Congregation.

RADIO AND TV

When the National Council of Catholic Men decided to sponsor the *Catholic Hour* Sunday evening broadcasts in cooperation with the National Broadcasting Company, Bishop Sheen became the first regular speaker on the program following the inaugural broadcast, March 2, 1930.

The program, which began on a 17 station network, was carried in 1950 by 118 NBC affiliates and by short wave around the world, with an average weekly listening audience estimated at 4,000,000 persons in the United States alone. The Bishop frequently received as many as 6,000 letters a day from listeners, about a third of them non-Catholics. Several million of his radio talks were distributed.

In 1940, Bishop Sheen conducted the first religious service ever to be telecast; the next year he served as narrator of the *March of Time* film, "The Story of the Vatican." Many transcriptions of his sermon have been made since an album of eight of them were recorded in 1946.

In the fall of 1951, Bishop Sheen began his "Life Is Worth Living" television series. By 1956, the Bishop was appearing on 123 ABC television stations in the United States alone (not counting Canada) and 300 radio stations. It was estimated that he reached 30,000,000 people each week. His "Life Is Worth Living" telecast has an audience of people of all faiths; and he received as many as 30,000 letters in one delivery; though normally, he averages from 8,000 to 10,000 letters per day.

He reaches millions of others through his writing, including the "God Love You" column, which appears in the Catholic press throughout the nation, and "Bishop Sheen Speaks," syndicated column for the secular press by George Matthew Adams Service, Inc. In addition, he is editor of *Worldmission,* a quarterly review, and *Mission,* a bi-monthly, which is the world's most widely circulated Catholic magazine.

On Labor Day, 1955, he became the first Latin Rite Bishop in history to offer a Solemn Byzantine Rite Mass in English. This he did at Uniontown, Pennsylvania, where more than 150,000 pilgrims joined him in praying for "Holy Russia." This event was beamed abroad by the Voice of America.

Bishop Sheen's "Life Is Worth Living" series terminated in 1957. His subsequent series on the life of Christ and a second series produced in 1964, "Quo Vadis America?", were shown throughout the United States until the appearance throughout the country in 1966 of "The Bishop Sheen Program" in color.

VATICAN COUNCIL II

Bishop Sheen was appointed originally to the Counciliar Commission on the Lay Apostolate for Vatican II. When the first session opened on October 11, 1962, he was unanimously elected to be a member of the Commission on the Missions. He was the only American on the Commission for the duration of Vatican II. He delivered an address in St. Peter's on the topic of the Missions on November 9, 1964 (during the third session).

In October, 1965, he returned briefly to the U. S. from Rome while attending the fourth session of Vatican II at the request of the CBS network, to be special narrator of Pope Paul VI's visit to the United Nations, the first time a Pope has visited the United States. Pope Paul VI reappointed him to the post-conciliar Commission on the Missions.

CONVERT INSTRUCTION

Bishop Sheen has spent more than 40 years instructing every type of convert. In 1965, he prepared 25 records on the Christian philosophy of life which have been issued under the same title of his television series, the LIFE IS WORTH LIVING SERIES. Each of the 50 talks runs about 30 minutes.

THE SOCIETY FOR THE PROPAGATION OF THE FAITH

It was announced on September 12, 1950 that Pope Pius XII had appointed Bishop Sheen head of The Society for the Propagation of the Faith, with the National Office at 366 Fifth Avenue, New York, N. Y. 10001. His work as National Director, for 16 years, spanned the reign of three Popes. Under his direction the U.S. was responsible for sending the Holy Father two-thirds of The Society for the Propagation fund collected from the entire world.

Founded in Lyons, France, in 1840, 'The Society for the Propagation of the Faith' is an international organization whose purpose is to further the evangelization of the world by united prayer and the collection of alms for impartial distribution among Catholic missionaries throughout the world. Its headquarters are in Rome under the direction of the Sacred Congregation de Propaganda Fide. There are approximately 150 diocesan officers of the Propagation of the Faith in the United States.

A Pontifical Society, the Pope has said that "all Christian

people should aid, through their generosity, the work of the Propagation of the Faith which of all the mission organizations is the principal one." (Rerum Ecclesiae).

None of the faithful, the Pope continued, either clergy or laity, "can claim exemption from this duty, *for this charity surpasses all other charity* as the mind surpasses the body; heaven, earth; eternity, time." (Rerum Ecclesiae).

As Communism swept across the face of the earth and Catholic Missions went up in flames, the burdens of the Propagation of the Faith became heavier; and the Holy Father turned his eyes and hope once more toward the United States for help which enables the Church to fulfill the command of Christ, "Teach all nations." (Matt. 28:19)

During 1949 an estimated 37,000,000 persons were being cared for by Catholic missionaries. In 1965 the number of Catholics alone being cared for by Catholic missionaries in mission countries, exclusive of Communist countries, totaled 44,741,087.

Today, depending upon the Propagation of the Faith are approximately 780 ecclesiastical territories, including archdioceses, dioceses and other church divisions, such as vicariates and prefectures apostolic. Approximately ¼ of these are presently under Communist tyranny.

ORGANIZATIONS

Organizations of which Bishop Sheen is a member include the American Catholic Philosophical Association, Mediaeval Academy, Catholic Literary Guild and the American Geographical Association.

AWARDS

Among the many awards received were the Emmy award in 1952 and the Look television award, received three different years. The University of Notre Dame conferred the Patriotism award on His Excellency; and the American Legion gave him the Golden Mike Award. For "outstanding achievement in bringing about a better understanding of the American way of life," he received the Freedoms Foundation Valley Forge award. For "outstanding achievement for the State, Church and University," he was awarded the Cardinal Gibbons award. He was the recipient also of the Catholic War Veterans Medal. He was made a Commander of The Order of the Crown of Belgium by King Baudouin in 1959. In 1964 he was presented The Order of Lafayette Freedom Award "for distinguished leadership in combating Communism."

Honorary LL.D. degrees have been conferred upon him by St. Viator College and Loyola University (Chicago) in 1929, St. Bonaventure (New York) College in 1939, and Notre Dame University in 1934; and that of Litt. D. by Marquette University in 1934; and that of L.H.D. by St. John's University (Brooklyn) in 1941. Georgetown University awarded him the Cardinal Mazalla Philosophy Medal in 1936.

Index

· · A · ·

ABELARD—525;
ABRAHAM—439;
ABUSE—1;
ACTION—593;
   Divine—282;
   Emotion—2;
   Thought—969;
ACTS
   Habits—3;
ADJUSTMENT—4;
ADVERSITY—5; 6;
ADVERTISING—262;
ADVICE—7;
AFFLICTION—8;
AFFLUENCE
   Problems—9;
AGE
   Old—10;
AGGRESSIVENESS—11;
AGNOSTICISM—12;
   Escapism—13;
ALCOHOLISM
   Cures—14;
   Drunkards—15;
   Love—16;
   Pride—17;
   Psychic Effects—18;
   Reasons—19;

ALCOHOLISM (Continued)
   Will Power—20;
ALIENATION—21;
   Modern Man—22;
AMERICA—434; 435;
   Communism—167;
   Decay—23;
   Good-Evil—24;
   Heritage—25; 303;
   Mission—26;
   Purpose—27; 28;
   Rights—851;
   Salvation—29;
AMERICANISM—30;
AMERICANS
   Abroad—31;
   Values—32;
ANARCHY—531;
ANGELS
   Belief In—33;
   Decisions—34;
   Intelligence—35;
ANGER—228; 385;
   Just Anger—36;
   Women—1030;
ANNAS—735;
ANONYMITY—37;
ANXIETY—38; 262; 354;
   595;

ANXIETY (Continued)
Cause—39;
Love—553;
Modern—40;
APATHY—41; 491; 674; 680;
APOSTLES' CREED—42;
APPEARANCE
Conscience—43;
Dress—44;
APPEARANCES—45;
APPLAUSE—46;
AQUINAS, THOMAS—79;
156;
ARGENTINA—707;
ARGUMENTS—47;
ARISTOTLE—525; 724;
ART
Artists—814;
Christian—48;
ASCETICISM
Egotism—49;
Love—50;
ASSUMPTION—51;
ATHEISM—52; 269; 1055;
Communism—53; 178;
Ego—313;
Intellectual—54;
Modern Atheists—55;
Religion—56;
Self-Hatred—57;
ATHEISTS—58; 869;
Energy—59;
Modern—55;
ATOMIC BOMB—60; 61; 1009;
Man—62;
ATOMIC ENERGY—63;
AUGUSTINE, ST.—708;
AUTHORITY
Educators—312;
Parental—64;

AVARICE—589;

·· B ··

BACH—669;
BAUDELAIRE—558;
BEAUTY—664;
Soul—65;
BECKET, ST. THOMAS A.—
527;
BEGET
Make—66;
BEHAVIOR
Children—100;
Doubt—67;
Growth—68;
Purpose—69;
Reputation—70;
BELIEF (See Faith)—339;
Negation—71;
BEREAVEMENT (See Death,
Grief, Sorrow)—72; 244;
BERGSON, M.—724;
BERKELEY—725;
BIBLE—391; 739;
The Church—73;
Soldiers—934;
BIRTH
Death—74;
BIRTH CONTROL—75; 76;
The Church—77;
BLESSINGS
Complacency—78;
BODY
Soul—79;
BOOKS—809; 810;
BOREDOM—80; 81;
Freud-Marx—82;
BOYS
Girls—83;

BRAIN WASHING—84;
BRAVERY
  Introspection—85;
BROTHERHOOD—86;
  Communism—87;
  Comraderie—88;
BUDDHISM—680;
BURDENS—89;

·· C ··

CAIPHAS—735;
CALAMITY
  Worth—90;
CALVARY (See Crucifixion-
  Cross)—634;
CAMUS—397;
CAPITAL
  Labor—91;
CAPITALISM—92; 774;
  Communism—181;
  Monopolistic—93;
CELIBACY
  Priestly—767; 768;
CHANGE—94;
CHARACTER
  Crisis—221;
  Environment—95;
  Experience—96;
  Psychology—97;
  Selfishness—98;
CHESTERFIELD—842;
CHESTERTON, G. K.—397;
  527; 726;
CHILDREN—99; 410; 411; 433;
  460; 477; 509; 510; 665;
  697; 816; 958;
  Behavior—100;
  Broken Homes—101;
  Development—102;

CHILDREN (Continued)
  Discipline—103;
  Duplicity—104;
  Education—304;
  Hatred—105;
  Parental Failure—106;
  Parental Training—107;
  Parent-Child Relationship—
    108;
  Parents—109;
  Rules—110;
  Sacrifice—861;
  Sensitivity—111;
  Teaching—112;
CHILDREN OF GOD—113;
CHILE—707;
CHOICE—366; 367;
  Cross—114;
CHRIST—115; 157; 238; 285;
  404; 405; 406; 408; 430;
  473; 494; 495; 497; 707;
  716; 750; 841;
  Body Of—116;
  Christ Of The Andes—707;
  Communion—165;
  Denial Of Existence—117;
  Good Man—118;
  His Death—119;
  History—120;
  Incarnation—121;
  Life—122;
  Love—557;
  Peter—723;
  Pre-Existence—123; 124;
  Pre-Historical—125;
  Savior—126; 496;
  Son of Man—127;
  Teachings—128;
  Truth Of—129;
CHRISTIAN ART—48;

CHRISTIANITY—130; 183;
    442; 1052; 1053;
    Corner Stone—131;
    East-West—132;
    Freedom—133;
    Politics—134;
    Russia—135;
    Secularization—136;
    Sinners—137;
    Supernatural—138;
    Virgin Mary—139;
    Western—140;
    World—141;
CHRISTIAN MORALITY
    Statistics—142;
CHRISTIANS—143; 380;
    Pagans—144; 692;
    Psychoanalysis—145;
CHRISTMAS—146; 147; 148;
    Good Will—149;
THE CHURCH—150; 155;
    866;
    Authority—151;
    Bible—73;
    Birth Control—77;
    Confession—190;
    Definition—152; 153;
    Enemies Of—154;
    Money—156;
    New Testament—157;
    Politics—733; 735; 736;
    Rebels—158;
    State—159; 310;
    Youth—1068;
CIRCUMSTANCES—160;
CIVILIZATION—161; 162;
THE CLOISTERED—163;
COLLEGES—947;
    Curriculum—164;
COMMUNION—165; 913;

COMMUNISM—166; 251; 285;
    369; 382; 471; 660; 709;
    712; 847; 854; 855; 856;
    857; 858; 859;
    America—167;
    Appeal Of—168;
    Atheism—53;
    Brain Washing—84;
    Brotherhood—87;
    Conscience—169;
    Economics—299;
    Hate—422;
    Individuals—170; 171;
    Injustice—172;
    Intellectuals—173;
    Language Of—174;
    Marxists—774;
    Mothers—175;
    Neurotics—176;
    Origin—177; 178;
    Purpose—179;
    Suppression—180;
COMMUNISTS
    Capitalists—181;
COMPANIONSHIP—182;
COMPARATIVE RELIGION—
    183;
    Philosophy—184;
COMPASSION—185;
    Involvement—186; 492;
COMPLACENCY—187;
    Blessings—78;
COMPLEXES
    Temptation—188;
CONDESCENSION—189;
CONFESSION—190; 551;
    Modern Man—191;
CONFLICT—192; 193;
    Inner—194; 195;
    Man—196;

CONFLICT (Continued)
  Tension—197;
CONFORMITY—198; 252; 474;
CONFUSION
  Personality—199;
CONSCIENCE (See Guilt)—
    413; 643; 644; 867; 931;
  Appearance—43;
  Communism—168;
  Denial Of—200;
  Examination Of—201; 202;
  Guilt—203; 412;
  Power Of—206;
  Science—205;
  Social Reform—928;
CONSOLATION—778;
CONTEMPLATION
  Meditation—206; 207;
CONVERSION—208; 209;
  Beginning—210;
  Converts—211;
  Moment Of—212;
  Sin—213;
  Understanding—214;
COURAGE—215;
COURTESY—216;
CREATION—217; 364;
  Creating—218;
CRIME
  Education—219;
  Law—220;
CRISIS
  Character—221;
  Men-Women—222;
CRITICISM—223; 761;
  Slander-Jealousy—224;
THE CROSS—229; 230; 285;
    291; 293; 297; 646;
  Choice—114;
  Crucifixion—225;

THE CROSS (Continued)
  Meaning—226;
  Sinners—227;
  Way Of—228;
CRUCIFIXION—225; 226; 227;
    228; 229; 230; 293;
CRUELTY
  Guilt—231;
CULTURE—232;
CYNICISM—233; 234; 235; 762;

· · D · ·

DANTE—525;
DEATH—236; 237; 464;
  Apathy—41;
  Birth—74;
  Christ—238;
  Fear—239;
  Immortality—240;
  Insensitiveness—241;
  Love—558;
  Loved One—244;
  Meaningfulness—242;
  Morticians—243;
  Preparation—245;
  Soul—939;
DEBAUCHERY—246;
DECADENCE
  Values—247;
DECISIONS—470;
  Angelic—34;
DECLARATION OF INDE-
    PENDENCE—248; 254;
DEGENERACY—246; 249;
DEGRADATION—246; 250;
    273;
DEMOCRACY—251; 253;
  Conformity—252;
  God-Given—254;

DEMOCRACY (Continued)
Issues—255;
Meaning—256;
DEPENDENCE—257;
DEPRAVITY—258;
DESCRIPTION—337;
DESIRE—259;
Carnal—260;
For God—261;
Satisfaction—262;
DESPAIR—263;
Criticism—223;
Eternity—264;
Misery—265;
Sin—266;
DESPOTISM—267;
DESTINY—268;
DEVIL—269; 270;
Description—271;
DIFFICULTY—272;
DIGNITY—273;
DISBELIEF—274;
DISCIPLINE—275;
Children—103;
Love—276;
Moral Force—277;
Obedience—278;
Parental—697;
Self—881; 882; 883;
DISCORD—279;
DISEASE—280;
DISOBEDIENCE (See Obedience-Discipline)
DISORDER—281;
DIVINE ACTION—282;
DIVINE LIFE—283;
DIVINE LOVE—284;
DIVINITY—498;
Love—560;

DIVORCE—419; 612;
Christ; Cross—285;
DOCTRINE
Method—286;
DOGMA—287;
DOSTOEVSKI—246;
DOUBT
Behavior—67;
DREAD (See Fear)—288;
DRUNKARDS (See Alcohol-ics)—289;
DUTIES—290; 457;

·· E ··

EASTER (See Resurrection)—
291; 292; 293; 294;
Giving—295;
Resurrection—297;
Victory—298;
Women—296;
ECONOMICS
Communism—299;
Modern—300;
ECUMENISM—301;
EDUCATION—302; 303; 772;
773;
Children—304;
Crime—219;
Ignorance—305;
Leisure—306;
Men, Women—307;
Philosophy—308;
Purpose—309;
Religious Schools—310;
Truth—311;
EDUCATORS—312;
EGO—313;
Heaven—450;
Hell—426;

EGOTISM—314; 448; 457;
  Asceticism—49;
  Greed—590;
  Psychosis—315;
ELEVATION—316;
ELIOT—397;
EMOTIONS—2;
EMPLOYMENT—317;
  Employees—774;
  Russia—318;
EMPTINESS—319;
ENEMIES—320; 561; 573;
  Love—321;
ENERGY—322;
  Atheists—59;
ENVIRONMENT—323; 476;
  562;
  Character—95;
  Responsibility—324;
ENVY—228; 325;
EQUALITY—326;
ESCAPISM—13; 327;
  Guilt—328;
ETERNITY (See Immortality)—
  329;
ETHICS
  Communism—174;
  Science—874;
EVIL—330; 399; 418; 603;
  Effects—331;
  Freedom—332;
  Hell—425;
  Love—333;
EVOLUTION—334;
  God—335;
  Grace—336;
EXPERIENCE—563;
  Character—96;
EXPLANATION—337;

EXPRESSION
  Self—885; 886;

· · F · ·

FAILURE
  Moral—670;
FAITH (See Belief)—126; 381;
  Acceptance—338;
  Belief—339;
  Gift—340;
  Loss—341;
  Nature Of—342;
  Reason—343; 344;
  Result Of—345;
FAITHFULNESS—346;
FALSE GODS—347;
FAMILIES (See Children, Parents)—348;
FATALISM—349;
FATHERS (See Parents, Children)—666;
FATIGUE—350;
FAULTS—351;
  Neighbors—352;
FEAR—239; 353; 358; 385; 490;
  595;
  Anxieties—354;
  God's Love—355; 356;
  Love—357;
  Terror—967;
FEMININITY—359;
FIDELITY (See Infidelity)
FLATTERY—360;
FLAUBERT—273;
FORGIVENESS—229; 361; 362;
  Redemption—363;
FRANCE
  Americans—31;

299

FRANCIS, ST.—212;
FREEDOM—364; 521;
  Christianity—133;
  Evil—332;
  License—530;
  Moral—365;
FREEDOM OF CHOICE—
  366; 367;
FREEDOM OF SPEECH—
  368; 369; 941;
FREEDOM OF WILL—370;
FREE WILL—371;
FREUD, SIGMUND—82; 372;
  905; 926; 1044;
FRIENDSHIP—373;
FRUSTRATION—374; 419;
  Causes—375;
  Individuals—376;
FUTURISM—377;

· · G · ·

GAMBLERS—378;
GIFTS—340;
  Giving—295; 379;
GIRLS
  Boys—83;
GOALS—775;
  Christian—380;
  Necessity—381;
GOD—382; 463; 599; 601; 602;
  608; 766;
  Evolution—335;
  Exile Of—383;
  Favoritism—384;
  Fear of—385;
  Image—66;
  Love Of—355; 356; 571; 574;
  575;

GOD (Continued)
  Man—386; 387; 388; 389;
  Man's Value—390;
  Science—871;
  Shouting—391;
  Truth—392;
  Will—1023; 1024;
  Worship Of—1057; 1058;
  Wrath Of—1059;
THE "GOD IS DEAD" MOVE-
  MENT—393; 394; 395; 652;
  780;
  Reflections On—395;
  Resurrection—398;
GOLD—671;
GOOD—603;
  Evil—399;
GOODNESS—400; 449;
  Hatred Of—401;
  Will—402;
GOSPEL
  Apostles' Creed—42;
  Mammon—403;
GRACE—232; 403-A; 404; 405;
  415; 656;
  Effect Of—406; 407;
  Evolution—336;
  Judgment—408;
  Life Of—409;
GRATITUDE—410;
GRIEF (See Death; Sorrow)
GROWTH—411;
  Behavior—68;
GUILT—203; 213; 230; 231;
  412;
  Escapism—328;
  Forms Of—413;
  Psychiatry—414;

·· H ··

HABITS—415; 416;
  Acts—3;
HANDSHAKE—417;
HAPPINESS—418;
  Wealth—419; 1018;
  Worldliness—420;
HARDY, THOMAS—397;
HATE (See Hatred)
  Answer—421;
  Communism—422;
  Love—423; 588;
HATRED—401;
  Atheism—57;
  Children—105;
  Enemies—320;
  Religion—825; 826;
HEAVEN—322; 424; 450;
HEIDEGGER—196;
HELL—314; 322; 425; 426;
  Denial Of—427;
  Earth—428;
  Love—429;
  Reality Of—430;
  Reason—431;
HEROD—735; 912;
HISTORY
  Christ—120;
HOLINESS
  Saints—432;
HOME
  Children—101; 433;
  Respect—434;
HOMES
  Broken—435;
HONOR—70; 436;
  Man—437;
  Reputation—438;
  Soldiers—935;

HOSPITALITY—439; 737;
HUGO, VICTOR—36;
HUMANISM—377; 440;
  Science—873;
HUMANITY—441; 565;
HUMAN RIGHTS—442;
HUMILITY—443; 444; 445;
  446; 764; 765; 776; 957;
  Discovery—447;
  Egotism—448;
  Goodness—449;
  Heaven—450;
  Meaning Of—451;
  Praise—452;
  Socrates—453;
HUMOR
  Laughter—520;
  Saints—454;
HUNGER—455;
HUXLEY, ALDOUS—680;

·· I ··

IBSEN—397;
IDEALS—456;
  Duty—457;
IDEAS—458;
  Truths—495;
IGNORANCE
  Education—305;
IMAGINATION—460;
IMMACULATE CONCEP-
    TION—461;
IMMORALITY—515; 531; 777;
IMMORTALITY—240; 329;
  462; 463; 467; 535;
  Denial—464;
  Mortality—465;
  New Birth—466;

IMPATIENCE—467;
INCARNATION—121; 468;
   717;
INDEPENDENCE—469;
INDIFFERENCE—251; 470;
   Socialism—471;
   Tolerance—472;
INDIGNATION—473;
INDIVIDUALISM—474; 475;
   Environment—476;
   Persons—477;
   Worth—478;
INDIVIDUALS—376; 629;
   Communism—170; 171;
INFALLIBILITY—479;
INFIDELITY—480; 614;
INFINITE—481;
INFINITY—482;
INJUSTICE—230;
   Communism—172;
INSENSITIVENESS—241;
INSTINCT—483;
INTELLECT—484;
   Religion—485;
   Truth—486;
INTELLECTUALS—12;
   Atheism—54;
   Communism—173;
INTELLIGENCE—487;
   Angelic—35;
INTELLIGIBILITY—488;
INTROSPECTION—201; 202;
   489; 894;
   Bravery—85;
   Fear—490;
INVESTMENT—317;
INVOLVEMENT—491; 930;
   Compassion—186; 492;

·· J ··

JEALOUSY—224; 493;
JEANS, SIR JAMES—545;
JESUS—494;
   Purpose—495;
   Savior—496; 497;
JESUS CHRIST
   His Divinity—498;
JOHNSON, DR. SAMUEL—
   842;
JOURNALISM—499;
JOY—500;
   Pleasure—501;
   Source—502;
JUDAS—323;
JUDGMENT—166; 408; 503;
   504; 567; 645;
   Human—505;
   Love—506;
   Man—507;
   Science—872;
   Self—891;
JUSTICE—508; 710;
JUVENILE DELINQUENCY
   —509;
   Affluence—9;
   Parents—510;
   Reason For—511;

·· K ··

KAFKA—397;
KENNEDY, JOHN F.—512;
   513; 514;
KIERKEGAARD—196;
KNOWLEDGE—515; 516; 517;
   814;
   Self—892;
   Unity—518;

·· L ··

LABOR—774;
  Capital—91;
LANGUAGE—519;
LAUGHTER—520;
LAW—529;
  Crime—220;
  Tradition—521;
LAWRENCE, D. H.—558;
LAZINESS
  Mental—522;
  Spiritual—523;
LEARNING
  Capacity—524;
  Desire For—525;
LEISURE—306; 526; 657;
LENT—527;
LIBERALS—528;
LIBERTY—248; 528;
  Responsibility—529;
LICENSE—530;
  Carnal—531;
LIFE—532; 533; 534;
  Divine—283;
  Future—535;
  Higher—536;
  Meaning—537;
  Meaninglessness—538;
  Pleasure—539;
  Purpose—540; 541; 542;
  Reason—543;
  Record—544;
  Romance—853;
  Spiritual—943; 944; 945;
  Thought—969 A
LIGHT—545;
LIKING
  Loving—546;
LIMITATIONS—547;
LINCOLN—514; 548; 841;

LISTENING—549; 636; 1063;
LONELINESS—550;
  Confession—551;
LOVE—298; 392; 552; 554; 562;
    563; 566; 571; 572; 576;
    581; 582; 583; 587; 588;
    605; 616;
  Alcoholism—16;
  Anxiety—553;
  Asceticism—50;
  Body, Soul—555;
  Carnal—556;
  Christ—557;
  Death—558;
  Depth Of—559;
  Difficulty—272;
  Discipline—276;
  Divine—284; 560;
  Enemies—321; 561; 573;
  Evil—333;
  Fear—357;
  Giving—379;
  Hate—423;
  Heart—564;
  Hell—429;
  Home—434;
  Humanity—441; 565;
  Judgment—506; 567;
  Like—546;
  Lovers—904;
  Loving—568;
  Men, Women—569;
  Mothers—570;
  Neighbors—677;
  Of God—575;
  Peace—711;
  Pleasure—732;
  Power Of—577; 745;
  Procreation—771;
  Reciprocity—578; 579;

LOVE (Continued)
  Sacrifice—580; 860;
  Self—893;
  Sex—584; 901; 902; 903;
  Sinful—585;
  Social—586;
  Suffering—950;
  Teenagers—960;
  Will—1021;
  Women—1027A; 1035;
  Work—1041;
  World—1046;
LUST—228;
  Avarice—589;
  Egotism, Greed—590;
LUXURY—591;
LYING—592;

· · M · ·

MACARTHUR, GEN.—757;
MAGDALENE—839;
MALRAUX, ANDRE—558;
MAMMON—403;
MAN—222; 281; 437; 596; 597;
    598; 599; 600; 604; 608;
    609 671; 681; 719; 815;
  Actions—593;
  Anxiety—595;
  Aspirations—596;
  Atomic Bomb—62;
  Change—94;
  Conflict—196;
  Education—307;
  Emptiness—319;
  Evil—603;
  Fear—595;
  God—386; 387; 388; 389; 601;
    602; 608;
  Good—603;

MAN (Continued)
  Humility—443; 447; 449;
  Infinity—482;
  Judgment—507;
  Love—569; 605;
  Modern—606; 607;
  Pride—766;
  Sex—905;
  Woman—605; 610;
  World—611; 1047;
MARRIAGE—613; 614; 615;
    616; 617; 618; 619; 620;
    621; 622; 623; 753; 777;
  Divorce—612;
  Infidelity—480;
  Selfishness—889;
  Sex—906;
MARTYRS—624; 625;
MARY—139;
  Virgin Birth—461;
MARX, KARL—82; 171; 196;
    475; 626; 627; 746; 926;
THE MASS—628; 741;
MATERIALISM—629;
MEDIOCRITY—633; 634;
MEDITATION—206; 207; 635;
    636; 637; 638; 639;
MEEKNESS—640;
MELANCHOLY—641; 642;
MEMORY—643;
MENTAL HEALTH—644;
MERCY—645; 796;
METHOD
  Doctrine—286;
MICHELANGELO—817;
MILITARISM (See Soldiers)
    —646;
MIND—647; 648; 649; 650;
MISERY—265;
MISSIONS—270; 651; 652;

MODERN AGE—653;
MODERN MAN—241; 245;
  262; 394; 593; 594; 595;
  596; 597; 598; 599; 600;
  601; 602; 603; 604; 605;
  606; 607; 608; 609; 610;
  611; 659; 703; 873;
  Alienation—22;
  Confession—191;
MODERN THEOLOGY—655;
MONEY—654; 656; 657;
  The Church—156;
MORALITY—365; 658; 659;
  660; 670; 773; 822;
  Statistics—142;
MORAL REGENERATION—
  8;
MORTICIANS—243;
MOTHERHOOD—359; 661;
  662;
MOTHERS—570; 663; 665;
  666; 667; 697;
  Beauty—664;
  Communism—175;
  War—1011;
  Women—1035;
MOTIVATION—668;
MUSIC—669;
MYTH
  Christianity—139;

·· N ··

NAPOLEON—757;
NATIONS—670;
NATURE—671;
NEGATION
  Belief—71;
NEGLECT—672; 673;
NEGLIGENCE—674;

NEIGHBORS—351; 352; 675;
  676; 677;
NEUROSIS—264; 679;
NEUROTICS—414;
  Communism—176;
NEW TESTAMENT—157;
  523; 934;
NIETZSCHE—395; 397;
NON-ATTACHMENT—680;
NOTHINGNESS—681; 682;
NUDITY—45;

·· O ··

OBEDIENCE—276; 683; 684;
  685;
  Discipline—278;
OBSCENITY—686; 739;
OBSCURITY—687;
OLD TESTAMENT—192; 523;
  934;
OPEN-MINDNESS—688;
OPINION—689;
ORIGINALITY—690;

·· P ··

PAGANS
  Christian—144; 692;
  Paganism—691;
PAIN—693; 694; 695; 696;
PARENTS (See Children)—
  510; 699; 700; 701;
  Authority—64;
  Children—109;
  Discipline—103; 697;
  Failure—106;
  Relationship—108;
  Teenagers—698;
PASSION—702;
PAST—703; 704; 758;

PATRIOTISM—572; 705;
PAUL—839;
PEACE—706; 707; 708; 709;
    710; 711; 712; 713; 714;
  Man—954;
PEACE OF SOUL—715;
PENANCE—580; 716;
PENTECOST—717;
PERFECTION—718;
  Imperfection—566;
  Man—719;
PERSECUTION—720;
PERSONALITY—199;
  Abnormality—722;
  Abnormal Person—721;
PETER—723;
PHILOSOPHERS—459;
  Bergson—724;
  Berkeley—725;
  Chesterton—726;
  Schopenhauer—727;
PHILOSOPHY—184; 728; 729;
    730; 731;
  Economics—300;
  Education—308;
  Political—735;
  Science—872; 874;
  Universities—997;
PILATE—230; 254; 735;
PLEASURE—500; 501; 539;
    694;
  Love—732;
POLITICIANS—163;
POLITICS
  Christianity—134;
  Church—733; 735; 736; 830;
  Religion—733; 736;
  War—1012;
POPULARITY—738;
  Religion—831;

PORNOGRAPHY—739;
POSSESSIVENESS—576; 740;
POVERTY—591; 737;
  Slums—741;
  Spiritual—742;
  The Poor—743;
  Wealth—744;
POWER—745; 779;
PRAGMATISM
  Marxism—746;
PRAISE—452;
PRAYERS—7; 747; 748; 749;
    752; 755; 756;
  Christ—750;
  Essence—751;
  Marriage—753;
  Schools—754;
PRE-EXISTENCE—123; 124;
    667;
PREPAREDNESS—757;
PRESENT—758;
PRIDE—36; 228; 759; 760; 776;
  Alcoholism—17;
  Criticism—761;
  Cynics—762;
  Docility—763;
  Humility—764; 765;
  Man; God—766;
PRIESTLY CELIBACY—767;
    768;
PRIESTS
  Preaching—769;
  Priesthood—770;
PROBLEMS—9; 620; 649; 908;
  Word—1049;
PROCREATION—771;
PROFESSORS—772; 773;
PROFIT-SHARING—774;
PROGRESS—775; 776; 806;
PROMISCUITY—777;

PROMISE—778;
PROPERTY—779;
PROTEST—780; 781;
PROVIDENCE—782;
PSYCHIATRY—414; 783; 784;
   785; 786;
PSYCHOANALYSIS—145; 787;
   788; 789;
PSYCHOLOGY—196; 231; 374;
   790; 791; 792; 793;
   Character—97;
PSYCHOSES—264;
   Egotism—315;
PSYCHOSYNTHESIS—794;
PUBLICITY—795;
PUNISHMENT—796; 797;
PURGATORY—798; 799;
PURITY—621; 771; 800; 801;
   802; 803; 1050;
PURPOSE—804;
   America—27; 28;
   Behavior—69;
   Communism—179;
   Life—540; 541; 542;
   Man—805;
   Progress—806;
   Youth—807;

· · R · ·

RACE
   Opinion—689;
   Racial Superiority—808;
READING—809; 810;
REASON—274; 431; 730; 814;
   844;
   Faith—343; 344;
   Grace—811;
   Judgment—812; 813;
   Men; Women—815;

REBELS—158;
   Rebellion—780; 816;
   Revolt—781;
RECLAMATION—817;
REDEMPTION—363; 817; 818;
   819;
   Self-Sacrifice—820;
   Strength—821;
REFORMERS—822;
RELIGION—827; 828; 829;
   833; 1052; 1053;
   Atheism—56;
   Communism—171;
   Comparative—183; 184;
   Cosmic—823;
   Divine—824;
   Dogma—287;
   Faith—339;
   Hatred—825; 826;
   Intellect—485;
   Politics—830;
   Professors—773;
   Sacrifice—832;
   Schools—310;
   Science—875;
   War—1012;
RELIGIOUS PERSECUTION
   —834;
REMORSE (See Sorrow)—835;
   836; 936;
REPRESSION—837;
   Christian—838;
   Zeal—839;
REPUTATION—438; 840; 841;
   Behavior—70;
RESPECT—434;
RESPECTABILITY—842;
RESPONSIBILITY—324; 843;
RESURRECTION (See Easter)
   —292; 294; 296; 297; 398;

REVELATION—844;
REVOLT—158; 780; 816; 781;
 845;
REVOLUTION—158; 780; 816;
 781; 845; 846; 847;
RIDICULE—848;
RIGHT
 Wrong—849; 850;
RIGHTS—248; 851;
RISK—852;
ROMANCE—853;
RULES
 Children—110;
RUSKIN—714;
RUSSIA (See Communism)—
 709; 712; 854;
 Christianity—135;
 Communism—178; 855; 856;
 857;
 Employment—318;
 Religion—858;
 Zeal—859;

· · S · ·

SACRIFICE—580; 832; 860;
 Children—861;
 Self—820;
SAINTS—432; 454; 581; 862;
 863;
SALVATION—695; 864; 865;
 866;
 America—29;
SANCTITY—702;
SARTRE, JEAN PAUL—397;
 681;
SAVIOR (See Christ Jesus)—
 292; 496; 497;
SCANDAL—867;
SCAPEGOATS—868;

SCHOOLS
 Morals; Religion—772; 773;
 Prayer—754;
SCHOPENHAUER—727;
SCIENCE—205; 545; 869; 870;
 871; 872; 873; 874; 875;
 Scientists—876;
SECULARIZATION
 Christianity—136;
SECURITY—877;
SCHUBERT—669;
SELF
 Alienation—21;
SELF-CONQUEST—878;
SELF-CONTROL—281;
SELF-DENIAL—529; 731; 879;
 880;
SELF-DISCIPLINE—881; 882;
 883;
SELF-DISCOVERY—884;
SELF-EXPRESSION—885; 886;
SELF-HATRED—893;
 Atheism—57;
SELFISHNESS—348; 582; 889;
 890;
 Character—98;
 Self-Interest—887; 888;
 Unselfishness—998;
 War—1013;
SELF-JUDGMENT—891;
SELF-KNOWLEDGE—892;
SELF-LOVE—893;
SELF-REFLECTION—894;
SELF-RIGHTEOUSNESS—
 895; 896;
SELF-SACRIFICE—820;
SENSITIVITY
 Children—111;
SERMON ON THE MOUNT
 —293; 634; 1050; 1054;

SEX—246; 376; 793; 897; 898; 899; 900; 904; 907; 1050;
  Love—556; 584; 901; 902; 903;
  Man—905;
  Marriage—906;
  Problems—908;
  Promiscuity—777;
  Science—873;
  Soul—909;
  Statistics—142;
  Victorians—1004;
SHAME—910;
SICKNESS—911;
SILENCE—373; 912; 913; 914; 915;
SIN—213; 230; 266; 797; 916; 917; 918; 919; 920; 921;
  Disbelief—274;
  Love—585;
  Selfishness—890;
  Sins—925;
  Thought—970;
SINCERITY—922;
SINNERS—15; 137; 227; 923; 924;
SLANDER—224;
SLAVERY—926;
SOCIALISM (See Communism)—267;
SOCIETY—376; 931; 932;
  Involvement—930;
  Social Reform—927; 928;
  Social Responsibility—929;
SOCRATES—305; 453;
SOLDIERS—933;
  Bible—934;
  Honor—935;
SONS (See Parents, Children) —667;

SORROW—72; 237; 244; 836; 936; 937;
SOUL—209; 259; 407; 630; 715; 938; 940;
  Beauty—65;
  Body—79;
  Death—939;
  Love—555;
  Sex—909;
SPEECH—368; 369; 915; 941; 942;
  Speaking—46;
SPIRITUAL LIFE—943; 944; 945;
SPIRITUAL PROFIT—946;
STATE—159;
  Schools—310;
STUDENTS (See Education, Teachers, Colleges; Universities, Youth)—947;
SUBJECTIVISM—948;
SUBLIMATION—316;
SUFFERING—7; 949; 950;
SUICIDE—233; 951;
SUPERIORITY—952;
SUPERNATURAL—138;
  Order—953;
SURRENDER—954;
SYMBOLISM—631;

· · T · ·

TALENT—322; 955;
TAOISM—680;
TEACHING (See Education) —957;
  Children—112;
  Teachers—956;
TEACHINGS
  Of Christ—128;

TEENAGERS (See Youth; Children; Parents; Discipline)—698; 958; 959; 960; 961;
TELEVISION—962; 963;
TEMPTATION—188; 964;
TENSION—194; 195; 197; 965; 968; 1056;
TERROR—967;
THEOLOGY—655; 786; 968;
THOUGHT
  Action—969;
  Life—969-A
  Sin—970;
  Thoughts—971; 972;
TIME—973; 974; 975; 976; 977;
TOLERANCE—472; 978; 979;
TOTALITARIANISM—281; 980;
TOYNBEE, ARNOLD—23;
TRADITION—521; 981;
TRAGEDY—982;
TRANSCENDENCE—983; 984;
TRANSFIGURATION—984;
TROUBLE—7;
  Tribulation—985;
TRUST—986; 987;
TRUTH—392; 459; 957; 988; 990; 991; 992;
  Christ—129;
  Education—311;
  God—989;
  Intellect—486;

·· U ··

UNITED NATIONS—739; 993;
UNITED STATES (See "America")

UNITY—518; 608; 609; 623; 937; 993; 994;
UNIVERSE—682; 995;
UNIVERSITIES (See Colleges; Education)—164; 772; 773; 947; 968; 996; 997;
UNSELFISHNESS—998;

·· V ··

VALUES—247; 390; 632; 1,000;
  Americans—32;
  Moral—999;
  Saints—863;
VANITY—1001; 1002; 1003;
VICES—250;
VICTORIANS—1004;
VICTORY—298;
VIRGIL—440;
VIRGIN BIRTH—461; 1005;
VIRTUE—70; 250; 818; 1006;
  Peace—706;

·· W ··

WAR—713; 1007; 1008; 1010; 1013; 1014; 1015;
  Atomic Bomb—61; 1009;
  Mothers—1011;
  Politics—1012;
WASHINGTON—548;
WEAKNESS—1016;
WEALTH—419; 744; 1017; 1018; 1019;
WHISTLER, J. M.—667;
WICKEDNESS—1020;
WILL—338; 370; 371; 402; 1021; 1022;
WILL OF GOD—1023; 1024;

WILL POWER
  Alcoholism—20;
WINE—1025;
WISDOM—1026; 1027;
WOMEN—222; 296; 569; 605;
    610; 815; 1030; 1031; 1032;
    1033; 1034; 1037; 1038;
  Education—307;
  Love—1027-A; 1035;
  Man—1028;
  Mothers—1036;
  Womanhood—1029;
WORDS—1039;
WORK—187; 1040; 1041;
WORLD—611; 845; 866; 1015;
    1042; 1044; 1045; 1046;
    1047; 1048; 1049; 1050;
    1051;
  Christianity—141;
  End Of—1043;
  Evil—330;
  Worldliness—420; 1053;
WORLD RELIGIONS—1052;

WORRY—350; 357; 1055; 1050;
WORSHIP—1057; 1058;
WORTH—478;
  Calamity—90;
WRATH—1059;
WRITING—1060;
WRONG
  Right—849; 850;

· · Y · ·

YEARNING—329; 481;
YOUTH (See Teenagers, Par-
    ents, Juvenile Delinquency,
    Discipline)—807;   1061;
    1062; 1063; 1064; 1065;
    1066; 1067; 1068; 1069;

· · Z · ·

ZEAL—839; 1070;
  Russia—859;

About the Editor

Frederick Gushurst, a native of Denver, Colorado, is a graduate of the University of Notre Dame (1946) and received his Master's degree in Philosophy from Columbia University. For the past five years he has been working on a major original philosophic essay: METAKINESIS—a new view of reality. A world traveler who served in the United States Merchant Marine, he now lives in Denver with his wife, the former Barbara Jean Hodkin, and their three daughters: Ann, Kristin and Bruna.

Quote

For 26 years QUOTE, The Weekly Digest for public speakers, has recorded the history of our times in the quotations of the men and women making that history.

Working with outstanding editors, the staff of QUOTE has published and indexed over half a million quotes, quips, and good stories representing the finest wisdom and wit of the past quarter century.

DATE DUE